Chronicle
of the year 1994

Chronicle
of the year 1994

Editor-in-Chief	Jacques Legrand
Editor	Andrew Hunt
Writers	Christopher Dobson, Peter Gordon, Perry Leopard
Database	Frank Breyten
Proofreader	Ingrid Shohet
Indexer	Irina Zarb
Production	Catherine Legrand assisted by Nadège Guy
EDP	Catherine Balouet

How to use this book

Chronicle of the Year 1994 reports the events of the year as though they had just happened.

The weekly chronology summaries do not aim to cover all the most important events since these are reported in greater detail in the reports adjoining the summaries. The summaries include less important events and those leading up to the main events reported elsewhere or their consequences. These chains of developments can be tracked through a system of cross-references that complements the index by pointing to the next link in the chain.

Arrows indicating the next link appear at the end of the reports or summaries. They point only forward in time, but can lead to either an entry in the weekly summaries or one of the fuller reports. They work like this:

• If a cross-referenced event occurs in the same month, only the day of that month will appear after the arrow – for example: (→15).

• If the next linked event occurs in another month, then the month will also appear – for example: (→15/3).

Where an arrow appears by itself after a weekly summary entry it means that the event and its consequences are reported in greater detail in the adjoining pages. Only one cross-reference appears per entry or report so the index should be used to find earlier entries on an event or individual.

First published in 1995 by
Dorling Kindersley Limited
9 Henrietta Street,
London WC2E 8PS

© Chronik Verlag
im Bertelsmann Lexicon Verlag GmbH,
Gütersloh/München, 1995

This edition copyright © 1995
Dorling Kinderlsley Limited, London

ISBN 0 75133 000 0

Colour processing by Valois Photogravure, Angoulême, France
Printed in England by the Bath Press

Chronicle
of the year 1994

DORLING KINDERSLEY

LONDON • NEW YORK
STUTTGART

January

1994

Brussels, 1
Greece takes over EU presidency.

Mexico, 2
Zapatista Army of National Liberation, made up of armed Indian peasants, seizes five towns in Chiapas. (→8)

Maracaibo, Venezuela, 3
105 people are killed in riots in one of Venezuela's largest prisons.

London, 4
In retaliation for the expulsion of the British ambassador from the Sudan, the Foreign Office orders the Sudanese ambassador to leave Britain.

London, 4
John Hume, leader of the SDLP, calls on the IRA to lay down arms. (→11)

Sarajevo, 4
Lieutenant-General Francis Briquemont, head of UN forces in Bosnia, is withdrawn at his own request. (→5)

Paris, 6
France sends home two Iranians wanted in Switzerland on charges of murdering an Iranian dissident; Zurich protests, saying Paris had promised to extradite them to Switzerland.

Kabul, 7
Factions agree to a one-day ceasefire after six days of fighting that has killed hundreds and wounded 3,000.

Tbilisi, 7
Georgian leader Eduard Shevardnadze confirms reports of the death of Zviad Ghamsakhurdia; the wife of the rebel leader said that he had committed suicide last December 31.

Houston, 7
Scotsman Andrew Devies is fatally shot after knocking at a door in a wealthy neighbourhood to seek help in calling a taxi; the owner took him for a burglar.

DEATHS

1. Cesar Romero, American actor (*15/2/07).

5. Thomas "Tip" O'Neill, former speaker of US House of Representatives (*19/12/12).

Environment Minister Yeo quits over affair with Tory councillor

His decision to resign came after his constituency leaders failed to back him.

London, Wednesday 5
Prime Minister John Major must be wondering what other disasters the new year has in store for him. His Environment Minister, Tim Yeo, has resigned following the revelation that he has fathered a child as the result of an extra-marital affair with Tory councillor Julia Stent. Yeo had been determined to hold onto his job but was forced into resignation when his South Suffolk constituency party called on him to reflect on the "widespread disappointment and criticism" over his affair. Tories fear this new debacle will bring ridicule on the government's "Back to Basics" family values campaign. (→10)

General Rose, SAS hero, appointed to lead UN forces in Bosnia

London, Wednesday 5
Lieut-Gen Sir Michael Rose, who masterminded the SAS assault on the occupied Iranian embassy in London and commanded the regiment, gun in hand, during the Falklands conflict, has been appointed to lead the United Nations forces in Bosnia. Sir Michael, presently commanding the UK Field Army, is expected to take up his duties in Sarajevo before the end of the month. His reputation as a fighting leader promises a more vigorous pursuit of UN operations. (→10)

January 4. Water, water everywhere, but the pub must not run dry: Torrential rains coming after the wettest December since 1979 have caused havoc on southern England's roads and misery for homeowners and farmers.

Johnners, the voice of cricket, has died

London, Wednesday 5
Brian Johnston, the irrepressible joker who brought his love and knowledge of cricket to millions with his commentaries, has died at 81. Tributes to him are pouring in. Prime Minister John Major said of him: "Brian was a giant among commentators. Over recent years he became almost the personification of cricket. He was a man who enjoyed life hugely ... Summers will not be the same without him."

"Johnners" was a man of many parts. He won the MC as a Guards officer during the war and used his rich voice to good effect on the popular radio shows *Down Your Way* and *In Town Tonight*. He also covered many of the big royal occasions, but it was in the cricket commentary box that he had most fun, bursting into uncontrollable giggles at some unintentionally risqué remark. Having made his love of cake known over the air, he was sent a constant supply by his women listeners. On hot days he washed his cake down with champagne. But through all the fun, he was the complete professional. "I understand there are some men who do not like cricket," he once said, "but I would not like my daughter to marry one." He was born on 24 June 1912.

'Womb-robbing' is to be investigated

London, Friday 7
The use of aborted foetuses to provide eggs for infertile women caused "unease, distaste and surprise" when it was first proposed to the Human Fertilisation and Embryology Authority, according to the authority's chairman, Professor Sir Colin Campbell. Launching a consultation document into the process today in response to public concern, Sir Colin said the authority, which licenses fertility clinics in Britain, was "impressed by what science could do but worried at the implications." He argued that people had to consider what the treatment would mean for any child born as a result of it and whether "our ability to manipulate the reproductive process is going beyond what is acceptable."

America's ice queen Nancy Kerrigan hurt in mystery crowbar attack

Detroit, Thursday 6
"God, why me? Why me?" cried figure skater Nancy Kerrigan as she collapsed to the ground after having been attacked by a man wielding a crowbar. The man smashed a plexiglass door that was chained shut and vanished into the stunned crowd. Kerrigan had been practising for tomorrow's national championships here. The skater was hit on the right knee, which is badly bruised; it is not known if she will be able to skate in the upcoming Winter Olympics at Lillehammer. (→ 21)

Zapatista rebels prepare to repel an army offensive in Chiapas

Mexico City, Saturday 8
Early this morning, a bomb nearly destroyed a parking garage here, reflecting the threat by the Zapatista National Liberation Army to bring its war to the capital. In the southern state of Chiapas, where the rebels have taken several towns, government troops are bombarding Zapatista strongholds, and the rebels are girding for an army offensive against them. The rebels are peasant descendants of the Maya, about 2,000 strong, and aim to retake their ancestral homelands. The government insists that the movement is led by radical Marxist groups that were active in the 70s. (→ 16/2)

The poorly armed Mexican guerrillas are led by 'Commandante Marcos'.

January 8. Pure perfection: Jayne Torvill and Christopher Dean, aged 36 and 35, win the British ice-dancing championship at Sheffield Arena, scoring an amazing set of nine perfect sixes for their free-dance routine.

January

1994

Su	Mo	Tu	We	Th	Fr	Sa
						1
2	3	4	5	6	7	8
9	10	11	12	13	14	15
16	17	18	19	20	21	22
23	24	25	26	27	28	29
30	31					

Bonn, 10
Bosnian and Croatian leaders agree to a ceasefire. (→19)

London, 10
Barclays Bank announces plans to cut 3,000 jobs by the end of next year.

Brussels, 11
NATO leaders endorse Clinton's Partnership for Peace plan for closer military cooperation with East European countries; they also renew threats of air strikes against the Bosnian Serbs.

Crossmaglen, Co Armagh, 11
An IRA bomb hidden in a van explodes at joint RUC and army base, seriously injuring two soldiers.

Washington, 12
Under criticism that he has not been forthcoming on the Whitewater affair, Clinton instructs Attorney General Janet Reno to appoint an independent counsel.

Italy, 13
Prime Minister Carlo Ciampi resigns, opening the way to new elections in the wake of the "Clean Hands" investigations. (→26)

Kenya, 14
Richard Leakey resigns from the Kenya Wildlife Service after Kenya's Tourism Minister announces an investigation into mismanagement and racism in the service. (→10/3)

Sandringham, 15
Queen Elizabeth II fractures her wrist in a riding accident; she is not seriously hurt but will wear a cast for several weeks.

Cardiff, 15
In a Five Nations Tournament international here, Wales defeat Scotland 29-6; in Paris, Ireland lose to France, 35-15. (→5/2)

DEATHS

12. Samuel Bronston, American filmmaker (*1909).

13. Johan Holst, Norway's Foreign Minister and architect of last year's secret PLO-Israel talks (*29/11/37).

14. Zino Davidoff, the "King of Cigars" (*1906).

15. Harry Nilsson, American singer-songwriter (*15/6/41).

Major's 'Back to Basics' crisis grows

London, Monday 10
The prime minister is desperately trying to patch together his crumbling "Back to Basics" campaign, which calls for a return to old-fashioned family values. He has just lost two ministers: Lord Caithness, who resigned following the suicide of his wife, and Tim Yeo, after the disclosure that he had a love-child by a Tory councillor. Westminster, a cruel gossip shop, is buzzing with stories of other sexual and financial improprieties. John Major called for an end to the moral witch hunt against Tories who had behaved foolishly. He said that Back to Basics was not about the sexual morality of individuals and has denied he was "preaching" at single mothers. The nation is not convinced.

The resignation of the Earl of Caithness came after his wife's shotgun death.

Scotland celebrates 500 years of whisky

And a wee dram for Sean Connery.

Scotland, January
In 1494, a clerk of the Scottish Exchequer noted a delivery of malt for the making of *aquavitae*. This is the earliest reference to whisky – the English transliteration of the Scottish word for water of life – to be made here, and this year is being celebrated as the soothing libation's 500th birthday. For lovers of this country's most famous export, the Scottish Whisky Association publishes a list of distilleries, 46 of which welcome visitors.

Sinn Fein ban lifted

Dublin, Tuesday 11
The Irish government lifted its long-standing broadcasting ban on Sinn Fein today and was immediately accused of making concessions to the IRA, which is still considering the Downing Street Declaration. The Rev Ian Paisley accused Dublin of playing up to the IRA, but this was denied by a government spokesman who insisted: "This is not part of any plan to woo Sinn Fein to the peace process." The ban remains in force in Britain. (→2/2)

Raging bushfires threaten Sydney and devastate local wildlife

Sydney, Monday 10
The capital of New South Wales has been smothering in a dark haze all weekend as 136 bushfires burned across 1.5 million acres of southeastern Australia. Although the fires are not all completely extinguished, authorities say they are under control, and the skies are beginning to clear. An estimated £200 million of damage has been done. Four people have died and thousands have been treated for smoke inhalation. Wildlife has suffered as well: Environmentalists say an entire generation of animals has been lost. Dry weather and high winds created the setting for the disaster, but police say they believe at least half the fires were set by arsonists.

For days, high winds have fanned the intense fire-storms around the city.

Royal first: Duchess of Kent becomes a Catholic

Westminster, Friday 14

The Duchess of Kent became the first member of the royal family to become a Roman Catholic in modern times tonight when she was received into the Church in a private ceremony by Cardinal Hume, Archbishop of Westminster. Watched by her husband and three children, who remain Anglicans, she solemnly declared her belief in Catholic doctrine and was anointed with blessed oil by the cardinal. Making the sign of the cross on her forehead, he said: "Katharine, be sealed with the gift of the Holy Spirit." The duchess, who consulted the Queen before converting, has been considering the move for several years. Her husband's place as 18th in line of succession to the throne is not affected.

After Mass the Duchess and her husband leave Cardinal Hume's private chapel in Archbishop's House, Westminster.

Senate investigates tragic radiation cases

Waltham, Mass, Thursday 13

Earlier this month, Ann Hopkins (left) and others demonstrated at the White House for compensation for US post-war nuclear testing practises. Today, a Senate committee heard testimony from two men who as students were fed radioactive substances without consent from them or from their parents. The experiment is among dozens revealed in Cold War documents ordered opened by Department of Energy Secretary Hazel O'Lear.

Clinton urges Yeltsin to continue reforms

Moscow, Thursday 13

At a champagne and caviar reception in the US embassy tonight, President Clinton urged President Yeltsin to carry on with his economic and political reforms. He did not offer a new aid package but pressed the need to control inflation and, instead of spending huge sums propping up inefficient state-owned properties, to spend more to help the victims of their restructuring. Yeltsin assured Clinton that his economic reforms would continue unabated and would be intensified in some fields despite his setback in last month's elections. The American president, anxious not to give Yeltsin's ultra-nationalist enemies any ammunition, took care at yesterday's welcoming ceremony to refer to Russia's greatness and portrayed Russia as an equal partner in a joint drive for global security and freedom. Tomorrow the two men are expected to announce that their nuclear missiles are no longer aimed at each other's countries.

Tory council accused of 'gerrymandering'

London, Thursday 13

In one of the most damning indictments ever delivered on a local council, the former leaders of Westminster City Council, headed by Dame Shirley Porter, were accused today of orchestrating a "disgraceful, unlawful and unauthorised" £21 million vote-rigging scandal. The accusations are contained in a report by the district auditor on the council's policy of selling council homes in eight key marginal wards which, it says, was designed to bring more Tory-minded voters into the area. Auditor John Magill said his view was that the council was engaged in gerrymandering.

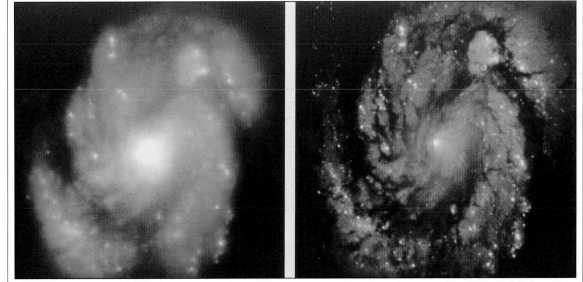

January 13. Here's looking at you: US space officials release dramatic before-and-after pictures of the M100 galaxy taken after the optics of the $1.6 billion Hubble Space Telescope, launched in April 1990, were repaired.

January

1994

Su	Mo	Tu	We	Th	Fr	Sa
						1
2	3	4	5	6	7	8
9	10	11	12	13	14	15
16	17	18	19	20	21	22
23	24	25	26	27	28	29
30	31					

Johannesburg, 16
The Pan-Africanist Congress says it is ending armed struggle.

Geneva, 16
Syria's President Assad tells Clinton he is committed to achieving peace in the Middle East.

Ho Chi Minh City, 16
Bryan Adams is the first Western rock star to give a concert in the Vietnamese capital since the war.

London, 17
John Major tells special inquiry he had no knowledge of relaxed government guidelines on sales of arms to Iraq in 1988-89.

London, 18
Prince Charles, who suffers from back strain, quits competitive polo.

Sofia, 18
Bulgaria's Supreme Court rejects appeal by former Communist dictator Todor Zhivkov against a sentence of seven years for embezzlement.

London, 19
Labour MP George Gallaway faces party disciplinary action after appearing on Iraqi television with Saddam Hussein; he is criticised for praising Saddam, but insists he only saluted the Iraqi people.

Vienna, 20
The International Atomic Energy Agency says North Korea has rejected visits to sites that the agency had demanded to inspect. (→ 3/3)

London, 21
Kelvin MacKenzie, editor of *The Sun* for 13 years, announces his departure.

Portland, Oregon, 21
Tonya Harding denies a claim by a former bodyguard that she helped plan the attack on Nancy Kerrigan. (→ 16/3)

Copenhagen, 21
Torvill and Dean win European ice-dancing championships. (→ 22/2)

DEATHS

20. Sir Matt Busby, football manager (*26/5/09). (→ 27)

20. Oginga Odinga, Kenyan opposition leader (*1911).

Major earthquake jolts Los Angeles before dawn, killing dozens

Los Angeles, Tuesday 18
Aftershocks measuring 4.7 on the Richter scale added further damage to the devastation caused by a 6.6-Richter-scale earthquake, which struck here yesterday at 4:31am local time. Motorways crumbled, water mains burst and flames spread throughout the area from the tremor which was centred in the San Fernando Valley at the city's northern limits. Property damage has been estimated in excess of $7 billion, and 34 people have died. It could take this urban region with a population of 9 million more than a year to repair the damage.

Pergau dam project at centre of storm

London, Tuesday 18
Controversy flared today over the Pergau dam project in Malaysia when Sir Tim Lankester, permanent secretary at the Overseas Development Agency, told the Commons Public Accounts Committee that John Major had overruled his warning that the £234 million British aid package was "unequivocally a bad one in economic terms and an abuse of the aid programme." (→ 2/3)

Muslims see red over Chanel bodice

Paris, Thursday 20
Muslim clerics have called for a boycott of the Chanel fashion house after supermodel Claudia Schiffer wore a low-cut dress with words in Arabic from the Koran printed on it. Today, Chanel dropped the dress from its collection, and designer Karl Lagerfeld apologised for the gaffe, adding that he had not known the writing was from the holy book – he thought it was a love poem.

January 19. Absolutely fab: Paul McCartney has confirmed reports that he, Ringo Starr and George Harrison are planning to record new songs.

Claudia flaunts the offending frock.

No progress made at new Bosnia talks

Geneva, Wednesday 19
The new round of talks between Bosnia's warring factions ground on fruitlessly today with no indication that peace was remotely possible. The only agreement, for Serbia and Croatia to open offices in Belgrade and Zagreb, served simply to further isolate the Muslims. Lord Owen, the European Union negotiator, took a cynical view of the agreement. He said that unless there was "a very dramatic change in the tone of the negotiations", Presidents Milosevic of Serbia and Tudjman of Croatia will go away "and fight one another at a terrible cost". (→ 28)

US feminists rejoice as Lorena Bobbitt is acquitted in penis case

The Ecuadoran-born manicurist leaves court at the end of an often lurid trial.

Manassas, Virginia, Friday 21
Lorena Bobbitt, the woman who cut off part of her husband's penis, was found not guilty by reason of insanity of "malicious wounding". She claimed that she had been driven to the act by years of abuse by her husband. John Wayne Bobbitt was acquitted last year of charges that he had raped her before the attack. Outside the courtroom, demonstrators showed their support for the 24-year-old from Ecuador, holding placards with slogans such as "We're with you, Lorena". The judge in the case ruled that she would have to be under observation for 45 days in a mental health facility because of the insanity finding.

'Who loves ya, baby?': Telly Savalas was Kojak for millions

Los Angeles, Saturday 22
Telly Savalas had a long and diverse career, but the Greek-American actor will be remembered as a tough New York homicide detective, Kojak. Born 21 January 1924, he made his first film in 1961 and was nominated for a best supporting actor Oscar in 1962 for *Bird Man of Alcatraz*. He first shaved his head for the role of Pontius Pilate in 1965's *The Greatest Story Ever Told*. He starred in *The Battle of the Bulge* in 1965, *The Dirty Dozen* in 1967 and *Kelly's Heroes* in 1970. He won two Emmys for the *Kojak* television series, which ran from 1973-1978. Savalas died today of prostate cancer.

Mighty Wigan team falls to underdogs

Headingley, Saturday 22
In one of the greatest upsets in the history of Rugby League, Castleford thrashed Wigan 33-2 to win the Regal Trophy here today. The mighty men of Wigan were stunned when Castleford came at them and beat them at their own relentless style of forward play, making two vital scores in the first 20 minutes. Their victory has prompted talk of the collapse of the established order, but it would be unwise to write off Wigan, they are still determined to win the Championship and Challenge Cup for the sixth successive year.

Romeo, O Romeo art thou too hetero?

London, Wednesday 19
The children of Kingsmead School in Hackney have been prevented from seeing a Covent Garden production of *Romeo and Juliet* because their headmistress, Jane Brown, objects to the ballet on the grounds that it is "entirely about heterosexual love." She turned down an offer by a charitable foundation to organize the outing, explaining that "until books, films and the theatre reflected all forms of sexuality, [she] will not be involving her pupils in heterosexual culture." Education Minister John Patten said her action was "crackpot".

January 22. Washington DC's homeless shelter from a cold wave that has killed some 145 Americans in a week.

January

1994

Su	Mo	Tu	We	Th	Fr	Sa
						1
2	3	4	5	6	7	8
9	10	11	12	13	14	15
16	17	18	19	20	21	22
23	24	25	26	27	28	29
30	31					

Britain, 24
In a television interview, Dame Barbara Cartland claims to have supplied John Major with the "Back to Basics" slogan; she got the idea, she says, from Margaret Thatcher.

London, 25
Joan Brady is the first woman to win the Whitbread literature prize, for *Theory of War*.

Italy, 26
Media magnate Silvio Berlusconi appears on his own television network to announce his entry into politics as leader of the centre-right *Forza Italia* grouping. (→ 28/3)

Denmark, 26
Europe's longest rail and motorway bridge, which is 6.6 kilometres long and links the islands of Fyn and Sprogo, is completed.

London, 27
The Public Accounts Committee publishes a report outlining 26 cases of government mismanagement and detailing the waste of hundreds of millions of pounds of public funds.

Brussels, 27
Lithuania becomes the first former Soviet republic to join NATO's Partnership for Peace.

Melbourne, 30
Pete Sampras beats fellow American Todd Martin, 7-6, (7-4), 6-4, 6-4 to win the Australian Open; yesterday German Steffi Graf defeated Spaniard Arantxa Sanchez Vicario 6-0, 6-2 to win the women's title.

London, 30
British Film Awards: Emma Thompson wins best actress, David Thewlis (*Naked*) is named best actor, and Ken Loach's *Raining Stones* is voted best film.

Algeria, 31
Defence Minister Liamine Zeroual is sworn in as president; he was chosen by the army-backed ruling council after Abdelaziz Bouteflika, chosen by a national conference, declined the post.

DEATH

23. Brian Redhead, BBC radio announcer (*28/12/29).

Prince of Wales barely flinches when assailant fires twice at him

Supt Trimming protects Charles (right) as security men grab the attacker.

Sydney, Wednesday 26
David Kang, an Asian student concerned about the plight of the Cambodian boat people, fired two blank shots from a starting pistol at the Prince of Wales as he was about to start a speech at an Australian Day celebration here today. As Kang, 23, scrambled onto the stage, he tripped over a microphone cable and was overpowered by Ian Kiernan, the round-the-world yachtsman. The prince was bundled out of harm's way by his bodyguard, Superintendent Colin Trimming, but remained as "cool as a cucumber" and within minutes was delivering his speech as if nothing had happened. The Australians are deeply embarrassed and a review of royal security has been ordered.

Terry Venables appointed as England coach despite controversy

London, Friday 28
Terry Venables has been appointed England's soccer coach in succession to Graham Taylor. It was by no means an easy decision. Venables, 51, is engaged in litigation over his dismissal as manager of Spurs, and there has been criticism of his business activities outside football. In the end, it was his reputation as a tactician and the esteem in which players hold him that won him the job. He said today: "We must go back to basics. I want to play good football but not fantasy football. We must have a system the players understand. It's up to me."

'EastEnders' star in High Court drama

London, Tuesday 25
Gillian Taylforth, star of the television soap *EastEnders*, collapsed in the High Court after she and her fiancé, Geoffrey Knights, lost their £500,000 libel action against *The Sun*. There was pandemonium in the court when the jury accepted police allegations published in the newspaper that the couple had been caught indulging in oral sex in their car on the A1. Members of her family shouted abuse at the court and reporters at the dramatic end of the trial, which has unrelentingly exposed the couple's personal lives.

Jan. 26. A dazzling exhibition of Fabergé eggs opens in London.

Michael Jackson to settle costly lawsuit

California, Wednesday 26
A civil suit charging pop star Michael Jackson with sexual molestation of a 14-year-old boy has been dropped. The lawyers for the boy and the singer did not reveal the details of their agreement, but it has been reported that Jackson will pay $5 million to settle the case out of court. Nevertheless, the Los Angeles prosecutors office is continuing its criminal investigation. The future of the case is uncertain, though, because minors involved in sex cases are not compelled to testify under state law.

Tears and rain at Old Trafford for Sir Matt Busby

Old Trafford, Thursday 27
The world of football paid tribute to Sir Matt Busby here today, home of his beloved Manchester United. A lone piper played a lament as the teams walked onto the pitch, and many of the spectators wept. Sir Matt, who died a week ago, created the club's great teams of the 50s and 60s, rebuilding after his magnificent "Busby's Babes" were destroyed in the Munich air disaster in 1958. Sir Matt barely survived the crash and was mentally marked by it for the rest of his life, but he was determined that his young players should not have died in vain and led their successors to triumph in the European Cup 10 years later. He was born on May 26, 1909.

Bosnia aid is halted after Briton's death

London, Friday 28
The British government suspended relief work in Bosnia today after Paul Goodall, 35, a driver with the Overseas Development Administration, was murdered by hijackers near the Muslim-controlled town of Zenica. Goodall, with Simon King, 27, and David Court, 42, was forced out of their Landrover and made to kneel on the river bank. The hijackers opened fire, killing Goodall with two bullets in the head. His friends, although wounded, jumped into the river and escaped. (→5/2)

£800 million sale of Rover to BMW provokes huge political row

London, Monday 31
The announcement today that Rover, the last British-owned car manufacturer, would be sold to BMW was met with protest from MPs and union leaders here and from Honda, which has a 20% stake in the company, in Japan. BMW will pay £800 million for an 80% controlling share in Rover. The Labour shadow Industry and Trade Secretary says that the company was sold at too low a price, £150 million, to British Aerospace when it was privatised in 1985. Honda's president says that the deal weakens Rover's brand identity as a British car. (→21/2)

Jan. 29. Steffi Graf celebrates her Australian Open victory. (→30)

Ulrike Maier killed in downhill-race fall

Germany, Saturday 29
Racing down the 2,685-metre course at Kandahar at about 60mph, two-time women's Super-Giant Slalom champion Ulrike Maier hit a soft patch of snow and lost control. Her helmet flew off when she hit a timing post and hurtled down the hill. Emergency workers tried to resuscitate the 26-year-old Austrian, but she was pronounced dead on her arrival at hospital. Her neck was broken and the main artery torn. Some skiers and coaches have criticised the conditions of the course as dangerous.

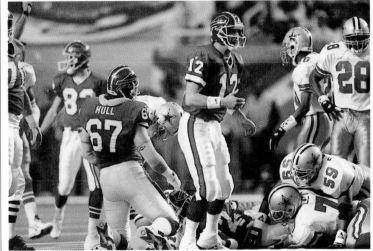

Jan. 30. A bad day in Atlanta for the Buffalo Bills, who fell to the Dallas Cowboys, 30-13. They are the only team to lose four straight Super Bowls.

February
1994
Su	Mo	Tu	We	Th	Fr	Sa
		1	2	3	4	5
6	7	8	9	10	11	12
13	14	15	16	17	18	19
20	21	22	23	24	25	26
27	28					

Bujumbura, Burundi, 1
In two days of clashes between Hutus and Tutsis, 50 people have been killed. (→ 7/3)

Algiers, 1
A French journalist of the Australian Broadcasting Corp is shot dead in a terrorist attack.

Washington, 1
Vice President Al Gore meets with Foreign Secretary Douglas Hurd to ease British anger over Gerry Adams's visit. (→ 2)

Egypt, 2
The Islamic Group tells foreigners to leave the country, warning of a "ferocious and strong" campaign against the government.

Erdut, Croatia, 2
Russian nationalist Vladimir Zhirinovsky says an upcoming test of the secret weapon "Elipton" will kill Bosnian Muslims with a lethal blast of sound.

Atlantic Ocean, 3
The bulk carrier *Christinaki* is swamped off Irish coast and sinks; all 27 crew members die.

Georgia, 3
Yeltsin and Shevardnadze sign a friendship and military cooperation treaty which brings Georgia back into the Russian sphere of influence.

Washington, 3
William J. Perry is sworn in as new US Defence Secretary.

China, 4
Three men imprisoned in connection with the Tiananmen democracy protests are released.

Britain, 4
British Coal confirms closure of four more pits, meaning the loss of 3,000 jobs.

Japan, 4
H-2 is launched; it is the first large rocket using only Japanese-developed technology.

Jackson, Mississippi, 5
Byron De La Beckwith, who had been acquitted by two all-white juries of the 1963 murder of black civil-rights leader Medgar Evers, is convicted and sentenced to life for the crime.

Dublin, 5
In a Five Nations match, Wales beat Ireland 17-15.

US–UK rift over Gerry Adams's visit

London, Wednesday 2
Sinn Fein chairman Gerry Adams has brought off a major propaganda coup in New York and seriously strained relations between London and Washington.

Downing Street had already summoned US Ambassador Raymond Seitz to protest about the granting of a visa to Adams, but nobody was prepared for the huge exposure he has been given on American television. Hailed as "an Irish statesman and former political prisoner", he has taken full advantage of soft questioning to project himself as a man of peace and to promote the IRA cause without once denouncing its campaign of violence. Members of the Clinton administration are dismayed by the media hype, and in an attempt to redress the balance, Vice-President Al Gore appealed for all parties to embrace the Anglo-Irish declaration. Prime Minister John Major, who condemned the "smoke screen of evasions and falsehoods" delivered by Adams in the US, is furious, fearing that Adams's coup will damage his peace initiative. The feeling in Whitehall is that President Clinton did not set out to antagonise Britain, but his decision to admit Adams signalled to Major that his views weigh far less on the president than those of the Irish-American politicians led by Senator Kennedy, who pressured him into granting Adams his visa – especially in an election year. (→ 19)

Unprecedented exposure in the New York media for the Sinn Fein leader.

February 3. From Russia with love: *Discovery* **blasts off at dawn carrying Sergei Krikalev, the first Russian to fly aboard a NASA space shuttle.**

Medicines cheaper in UK, report says

Washington, Wednesday 2
Top-selling brand-name drugs are much more expensive in the United States than in Britain, says the US General Accounting Office. Six out of seven prescribed drugs sold in both countries cost more here, most more than twice as much. One of the more extreme examples is the contraceptive Nordette, which is 17 times more expensive in the US.

Congressman Henry Waxman requested the report as Americans debate the reform of their health-care system. The study gives ammunition to those calling for regulation of the pharmaceutical industry.

Sarajevo atrocity: Mortar shell kills 68 in market

Bosnia, Saturday 5
There were scenes of carnage at Sarajevo's central market today when a single mortar bomb slaughtered 68 people and wounded nearly 200. The attack came without warning, and the 120mm shell landed in the centre of the crowded market. The effect was devastating, with shrapnel slicing through the stalls. Sir Michael Rose, the British commander of UN troops here, said it was technically impossible to say where the bomb came from, but the people of Sarajevo are in no doubt: it was the Serbs, their former neighbours, who now command the hills above the city. The massacre has been swiftly condemned by world leaders. President Clinton has summoned an emergency meeting of his crisis team, while Britain and France have called for an urgent meeting of NATO to consider a military response. (→9)

Hanoi embargo over

Washington, Thursday 3
President Clinton today ended the US economic embargo against Vietnam, which has been in effect since the end of the war in 1975. The president said he intends to take steps toward establishing diplomatic relations with the Southeast Asian country but reiterated concern about the US soldiers still missing and unaccounted for from the war.

Portillo apologises

London, Friday 4
Gaffe-prone Michael Portillo, Chief Secretary of the Treasury, was today forced to apologise after a speech attacking standards of public life abroad. He told an audience of students: "If any of you have got an A level it is because you have worked to get it. Go to any other country, and when you have got an A level you have bought it."

Callard kick wins it

Murrayfield, Saturday 5
Scotland lost the Calcutta Cup with the last kick of the match here today. All Scotland thought their team had won when they took the lead at the end of normal time, but then, with injury time ticking away, England gained a penalty. Nerveless Jon Callard stepped up to stroke the ball home, winning the match for England, 15-14. (→19)

Nude man on palace

London, Saturday 5
The Fan Man has struck again, this time at Buckingham Palace. James Miller, a 30-year-old American, flew toward the palace in his motorised paraglider, a navigable parachute with a small petrol engine attached. He landed on the roof, took off his clothes to reveal his naked body painted green from the waist down and was promptly arrested.

Feb. California dreamin': The world's biggest Harley, a 650hp, four-ton behemoth that seats six, has a jacuzzi and can be rented for £2,500 a day.

© Walt Disney

February 2. Disney's new full-length cartoon, *The Lion King*, with Jeremy Irons as the evil uncle Scar and songs by Elton John, opens in New York.

February
1994

Su	Mo	Tu	We	Th	Fr	Sa
		1	2	3	4	5
6	7	8	9	10	11	12
13	14	15	16	17	18	19
20	21	22	23	24	25	26
27	28					

Costa Rica, 6
José Maria Figueres, the opposition candidate, is elected president.

Finland, 6
Social Democrat Martti Ahtisaari is elected president.

London, 7
The High Court bans *Maxwell: the Musical* because of the "risk of serious prejudice" to the trial of Kevin and Ian Maxwell.

London, 8
The government cuts minimum lending rate to 5.25%, lowest since 1972.

London, 8
Chatset, the independent Lloyd's analyst, estimates 1991 losses at £2.05 billion and advises Names to accept the Lloyd's settlement offer.

London, 9
Labour's leading anti-European MP, Brian Gould, retires.

London, 10
Three men are jailed in connection with last year's IRA bombing of Warrington gasworks: Pairic MacFhloinn is sentenced to 35 years and Denis Kinsella to 25 years for the bombing, and John Kinsella is sentenced to 20 years for possessing Semtex.

Britain, 11
In a contest sponsored by Cadbury's and *She* magazine, Anthony Abbott, who proposed to his girlfriend by having "Will you marry me?" flashed on the scoreboard at a Plymouth Argyle match, is named Britain's most romantic man; the couple are now married.

London, 11
John Cahill, executive chairman of British Aerospace, announces retirement; he is leaving with a compensation package worth more than £3 million.

DEATHS

6. Gwen Watford, British actress (*10/9/27).

6. Joseph Cotten, American actor (*15/3/05).

11. William Conrad, American actor (*27/9/20).

12. Sir Vincent Wigglesworth, British biologist (*17/4/99).

Tory MP Stephen Milligan's macabre death stuns Conservatives

The 45-year-old politician was considered to be a rising star in the Tory party.

London, Tuesday 8
The Conservative Party is shocked by the bizarre death of Stephen Milligan, an able and ambitious politician. Milligan, the bachelor MP for Eastleigh, was found in the kitchen of his London home by his secretary yesterday afternoon after he had failed to keep some appointments. He was naked apart from a pair of stockings and a suspender belt and had a cord round his neck.

A journalist before he entered parliament in 1992, he had recently been appointed parliamentary private secretary to Jonathan Aitken at the defence ministry. Police are treating his death as "suspicious", but the indications are that he was engaged in a sexual act which went horribly wrong.

Tension high as Sarajevo marks 10th anniversary of Olympics

Sarajevo, Wednesday 9
An uneasy calm has come to this battered city after the Serb besiegers caved in to a NATO ultimatum to withdraw their heavy weapons 13 miles from the city centre or face air strikes. This time there could be no doubt that NATO, shocked by the mortar massacre in the central market last Saturday, means to take action. Apart from the human suffering wrought by the Serbian guns, one of the most poignant victims of their shells is the wrecked stadium where the Winter Olympics were held 10 years ago this week. (→ 18)

February 10. Picasso's daughter, Paloma, gets ready for next week's opening of an exhibition of the artist's work at the Tate.

India's Kapil Dev breaks cricket record

Ahmedabad, Tuesday 8
When Indian all-rounder Kapil Dev had Sri Lankan batsman Hashan Tillekeratne caught at forward short leg here today, the crowd went wild, his teammates rushed to congratulate him and 432 balloons soared into the air, for Kapil had just taken his 432nd Test wicket and broken the record set by New Zealander Sir Richard Hadlee. Kapil, 35, owes his success to his resilience as well as his skill: He has missed only one Test since making his debut 16 years ago. He says his aim now is to take 475 Test wickets before he retires. A target of 450 may be more realistic.

Feb. 10. Prince Charles relaxes at the end of a New Zealand tour, three days after an anti-royalist sprayed him with an aerosol.

US auto giants plunge back into the black

General Motors announces its first quarterly profit after four disastrous years.

New York, Thursday 10
The Big Three US automobile manufacturers have all posted healthy profits for last year. The smallest of the trio, Chrysler, set a company record of $2.4 billion in profits, Ford announced profits of $2.53 billion, and GM, the largest US carmaker, posted $2.5 billion. Last year, Ford and GM posted record losses. Most of the money was made in the home market; the improved US economy and lower interest rates made 1993 a bonanza year for car sales, while Europe remained much less profitable. Cost cutting – retiring overlapping plants and reducing the workforce – has been a major goal in the automobile industry.

Cartoonist Calman dies during a film

London, Thursday 10
Mel Calman died of a heart attack tonight in a Leicester Square cinema during the film *Carlito's Way. The Times* front page cartoonist for the past 15 years, Calman was born in north London on May 19, 1931.

His droll, primitively sketched one-frame drawings manifested an absurd view of life and an affinity for the underdog. He was the founder of the Cartoon Gallery, which aims to bring recognition and financial reward to cartoonists.

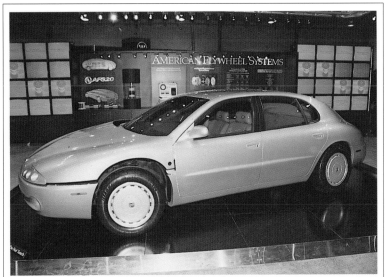

February 12. The AFS20, a $30,000 electric car equipped with a flywheel battery, is one attraction at the Los Angeles Ecological Auto Show.

Hail of bullets kills 'Mad Dog' terrorist

Drogheda, Thursday 10
Dominic "Mad Dog" McGlinchy, who boasted of carrying out 30 murders, was mown down by three gunmen here today as he used a public phone box next to the town's hospital. McGlinchy was marked for death by his violent rule as leader of the extremist Irish National Liberation Army, a breakaway group from the IRA. Shortly before his death, he said he knew he was being stalked by a family determined to kill him to settle a 10-year-old feud. In 1987, while he was in prison, his wife and fellow extremist, Mary, was shot dead as she bathed their sons. The oldest boy, Dominic, 16, has seen both his parents die.

Munch masterpiece stolen from gallery

Oslo, Saturday 12
Lax security is being blamed for the theft of what is perhaps Norway's most famous work of art – Edvard Munch's depiction of an anguished person, hands on the head, emitting a painful cry. *The Scream* was stolen from the National Art Museum here by thieves who simply broke a window, climbed through and snatched the painting from a collection celebrating Norwegian culture mounted in connection with the Winter Olympics in Lillehammer.

The Scream, or *Skriet* in Norwegian, was painted in 1893 as a part of Munch's *The Frieze of Life* series, in which he explored the themes of sickness, anxiety and love.

February 12. As sportsmen from 69 nations, 40,000 spectators and tens of millions of TV viewers looked on, the XVIIth Winter Olympics got off to a spectacular start. Veteran ski jumper Stein Gruben, carrying a five-foot torch, made a perfect jump. The torch was then handed to Norwegian Crown Prince Haakon, who lit the huge cauldron to open the Games.

February
1994

Su	Mo	Tu	We	Th	Fr	Sa
		1	2	3	4	5
6	7	8	9	10	11	12
13	14	15	16	17	18	19
20	21	22	23	24	25	26
27	28					

London, 13
Hartley Booth, Tory MP and part-time Methodist minister, resigns from his Foreign Office post after allegations of an affair with a female researcher.

Ghana, 13
More than 1,000 people have died and 70 villages have been razed in fighting between ethnic groups.

Iran, 14
After John Major calls for lifting of death edict on Salman Rushdie, Iran restates the call for his death.

London, 14
In a single day, George Soros's Fund Management loses $600 million in currency markets due to the dollar's plunge against the yen and the drop in the Tokyo stock market.

Scotland, 15
Rescue teams find Jacqueline Greaves, aged 53, alive after having endured wind-chill temperatures of -26ºC for two nights in a sleeping bag; she had been caught in a blizzard while climbing Derry Cairngorm mountain.

Indonesia, 16
An earthquake measuring 6.5 on the Richter scale strikes the island of Sumatra; at least 184 people are killed.

Barbados, 16
England score 202 for five, then bowl out the West Indies for 141 with nine overs remaining in the first one-day Test match of their West Indian tour.

Mexico, 16
The former governor of Chiapas state, kidnapped February 2 by the Zapatista Army of National Liberation, is freed by the rebels. (→ 21)

Athens, 17
Greece closes its border with Macedonia in an effort to push the country to change its name, flag and constitution.

Belfast, 18
Loyalist gunmen kill three workmen outside Sinn Fein headquarters.

DEATH

19. Derek Jarman, British filmmaker (*1942).

The Queen agrees to visit Russia this year, Major tells Yeltsin

The Russian leader wants the royal visit to take place before the end of 1994.

Moscow, Wednesday 16
The Queen is to visit Russia later this year and so heal the long rift caused by the Bolshevists' murder of Tsar Nicholas and his family, who were distant but fond relatives of the British royal family. The Queen's grandfather, George V, was a cousin of the Tsar, and the Tsarina was Prince Philip's great-aunt. John Major broke the news to Boris Yeltsin that the Queen had accepted his invitation as he left the Kremlin tonight to continue his tour of Russia. The prime minister said the royal visit would "set the seal" on Western recognition of the steps Russia has taken towards democracy and economic reform since the collapse of communism.

Huge breast implant settlement is agreed

Birmingham, Alabama, Monday 14
The largest US producers of silicone breast implants – Dow Corning, Bristol-Myers Squib and Baxter International – have agreed to pay most of a $4.75 billion settlement proposed by lawyers representing thousands of women who have been harmed by the implants. Lawsuits against 20 companies have been consolidated in the federal court district here. Breast implants can rupture and leak, and they have been blamed for ailments such as disorders of the immune system. Women would be compensated for injury as well as discomfort and disfigurement.

Burmese dissident to be detained till 1995

Rangoon, Tuesday 15
Burmese dissident and Nobel Peace Prize winner Daw Aung San Suu Kyi has rejected an offer from the government to free her if she leaves the country. "That is never going to happen," she said. On Monday, a foreign delegation was allowed to meet with her; they were her first visitors, apart from her family and doctors, since she was put under house arrest on July 20, 1989. The National League for Democracy, which she led before her arrest, won a landslide victory in 1990 elections; the government subsequently arrested most of the party's other leaders. A senior junta official said today that Aung San Suu Kyi would stay under house arrest until 1995.

February 14. Bjork is best international female singer at the Brit Awards, at Alexandra Palace.

Viacom wins bitter US takeover battle

New York, Tuesday 15
The battle of the communications giants has ended. After five months of offers and counter-offers, Paramount shareholders have voted to accept Viacom's $9.8 billion merger plan over that of QVC. The deal will create one America's largest media empires. Paramount owns a movie studio, a television programming library and other entertainment and publishing concerns. Viacom operates cable television companies such as MTV and Nickelodeon.

Europol is open for business in Holland

The Hague, Wednesday 16
Herr Jurgen Storbeck, former German head of Interpol, today launched Europol, a prototype European Union police force. Speaking at the former offices of the Dutch secret service, Storbeck spoke of his ambition to enforce the law across the EU, ignoring national borders. "I think governments will agree to this federal ideal," he said. "What was unthinkable 10 years ago has now become thinkable." He is planning Europe-wide databanks on crime.

Serbs gradually pull back as NATO forces prepare for air strikes

NATO reconnaissance photographs clearly show Bosnian Serb heavy artillery positioned around the Bosnian capital.

Sarajevo, Friday 18
The Serbian forces around Sarajevo are reluctantly pulling back their tanks and heavy guns under threat of attack by NATO warplanes.

Slowed by snow and a lack of transport as well as their reluctance, it is unlikely they will meet tomorrow's deadline. This does not mean, however, that they will inevitably be bombed. Officials agree that the point of the ultimatum is to stop the shelling of Sarajevo, and as long as the ceasefire holds, the UN is unlikely to sanction air strikes even if Serbian heavy weapons remain within the 13-mile exclusion zone. Meanwhile a company of Grenadier Guards has arrived to take charge of guns left behind by the Serbs. (→ 28)

IRA bombs West End as premiers meet

London, Saturday 19
Albert Reynolds, the Irish prime minister, and John Major talked peace for 90 minutes at Downing Street today against a background of IRA firebombs in seven central London stores which caused thousands of pounds worth of damage. After the meeting, Reynolds gave his officials the go-ahead to begin talks with their British counterparts to thrash out some of the "notions" floated by Sir Patrick Mayhew, the Northern Ireland secretary, earlier this month. Before leaving with Reynolds to watch the England v Ireland rugby international, Major said: "No one should be able to veto progress on the talks. We have made clear what Sinn Fein need to do to join." (→ 28)

Phoolan Devi, India's legendary Bandit Queen, is freed at last

The police say she began killing after being raped by a gang of robbers.

New Delhi, Friday 18
One of the most notorious women in India has been released after 11 years in jail. Phoolan Devi, who is called the Avenging Angel, the Rebel of the Ravines and the Bandit Queen, is a hero to many lower-caste Indians. She was born into the Mallah caste of fisherman, close to the bottom of India's rigid social scale. She became a bandit after she was raped and led her rural gang in killings of upper-caste Thakurs to get revenge for the murder of her lover. Now free, she says she will "work for the upliftment of women and the downtrodden".

Feb. 17. Salman Rushdie attends premiere of *Schindler's List*.

The underdogs win in London, Cardiff

London, Saturday 19
It was a day of upsets in the Five Nations Tournament. At Twickenham, the Irish held on to a halftime lead to defeat the English, 13-12, for the first time since 1982. In Cardiff, the Welsh, who finished at the bottom of the pile in last year's tournament, stunned the French in a 24-15 win. The French captain was magnamimous, saying: "It's good for rugby that they are back." Only Wales now have a possibility of completing the Grand Slam. (→ 5/3)

February 19. Despite opposition from French and Pentagon officials, American D-Day veterans plan to hit the Normandy beaches on June 6.

February

1994

Su	Mo	Tu	We	Th	Fr	Sa
		1	2	3	4	5
6	7	8	9	10	11	12
13	14	15	16	17	18	19
20	21	22	23	24	25	26
27	28					

Switzerland, 20
Voters pass ban on foreign lorries crossing the country by road, to be fully effective within 10 years.

Tokyo, 21
Honda announces it is ending its investment in Rover.

Berlin, 21
In the Name of the Father wins the Golden Bear at the Berlin Film Festival; Crissy Rock is named best actress for *Ladybird, Ladybird*.

Mexico, 21
Peace talks begin between the government and Zapatista rebels. (→ 3/3)

Britain, 23
After the decision by the Church of England to ordain women priests, seven bishops and more than 700 clergy announce plans to become Roman Catholic. (→ 12/3)

New York, 24
Bell Atlantic Corp and Tele-Communications Inc drop their plans to join forces in what would have been the largest telecom merger ever.

London, 25
Granada succeeds in a £771 million takeover bid for London Weekend Television.

London, 25
Ian Holme (*Moonlight*) and his wife Penelope Wilton (*Deep Blue Sea*) are named best actor and actress in the London Critics' Drama Awards; Tom Stoppard's *Arcadia* is best play.

Jamaica, 26
In second Test, West Indies score 240 for 7 in 45.5 overs against England's 253 for 8 in 50 overs.

Belfast, 28
The Ulster Unionist Party says it will not participate in peace talks with the British and Irish governments and local parties in Northern Ireland. (→ 1/3)

DEATHS

22. "Papa" John Creach, American rock and blues violinist (*28/5/17).

24. Dinah Shore, American actress and singer (*1/3/18).

27. Sir Harold Acton, British author and historian (*1905).

MPs vote for a lower gay age of consent

As MPs vote, angry gay rights militants clash with police outside Westminster.

London, Monday 21
Gay rights activists clashed with police outside parliament last night while an impassioned debate inside the Commons ended with the lowering of the age of consent for homosexuals from 21 to 18. MPs voted by a majority of 265 for the first change in the law on homosexuality in 27 years. However, the activists, who had mounted a candlelit vigil, were infuriated when they learnt that a more radical proposal to equalise the age of consent for homosexuals and heterosexuals had been turned down after Michael Howard, the home secretary, said there was a need to protect young men "from activities which their lack of maturity might cause them to regret". Activists called the MPs "gutless cowards" and vowed to continue campaigning for equality with "suffragette-style protests".

Britons furious over Torvill-Dean verdict

Lillehammer, Tuesday 22
The whole of Britain is convinced that Jayne Torvill and Christopher Dean were robbed of the Olympic Gold Medal for ice dancing last night. They took the bronze with their new routine *Let's Face the Music and Dance*. Spectators whistled derisively at the marks given to the couple, who had returned to the amateur ranks in their attempt to win the title they had last won in Sarajevo a decade ago. Dean said: "We should have done a much more emotional routine." (→ 2/3)

CIA masterspy Ames is belatedly caught

Washington, Tuesday 22
The former head of the CIA's Soviet counterintelligence branch and his wife were charged today with spying for Russia for nearly 10 years. Aldrich and Rosario Ames began making mysterious large bank deposits in 1985; the KGB is said to have paid Ames a total of $1.5 million. The Justice Department is calling this one of the biggest espionage cases ever. (→ 28/4)

February 22. Tens of millions of gallons of thick black mud and water pour out of a burst earthen gold-mine dam near Virginia, approximately 120 miles south-west of Johannesburg, killing an estimated 45 local inhabitants.

Bloodbath in West Bank

Nervous Israeli police on patrol near the Tomb of the Patriarchs in Hebron.

Hebron, Friday 25
Riots are raging throughout the Israeli occupied territories after a gunman shot down 30 worshippers in a mosque here today. Dr Baruch Goldstein entered the Ibrahim mosque near the Tomb of the Patriarchs, said to be the burial site of Abraham and holy to both Jews and Muslims, to unleash the worst bloodshed since the 1967 war. He placed himself in the only door of a prayer room measuring 70 by 90 feet and opened fire with an automatic assault rifle on the kneeling worshippers. It is feared the massacre may do great damage to the Israeli-Palestinian peace process. Prime Minister Rabin called the killings a "loathsome criminal act". President Clinton announced that negotiators had agreed to return to Washington as soon as possible to continue their work. (→ 5/3)

Texas jury acquits four Waco cultists

San Antonio, Saturday 26
A Texas jury has handed down a mixed verdict on 11 followers of David Koresh who were in his sect's headquarters when four federal agents were killed in a raid on the ranch last year. Four defendants were acquitted on all charges; five were convicted of aiding and abetting manslaughter and two of firearms violations. The decision is seen as a sharing of responsibility for the deaths in the raid and in the following razing of the ranch that killed Koresh and many of his followers.

Coup leaders freed, setback for Yeltsin

Moscow, Saturday 26
The leaders of last October's uprising walked out of prison today, freed by a sweeping amnesty declared by parliament, leaving President Yeltsin, who had failed in a last minute attempt to have the amnesty declared illegal, humiliated and vulnerable. As he left prison, Aleksandr Rutskoi, former vice-president and leader of the revolt, vowed to challenge Yeltsin for the presidency.

Murder house man jailed in Gloucester

Gloucester, Monday 28
Frederick West, a 52-year-old builder, was charged with the murder of his daughter, Heather, last night after her remains were found in the garden of his home. Heather was last seen alive six years ago. She was then 16. The discovery follows three days of excavation in which

The gruesome police search goes on.

the police have used mini-diggers in the small garden of West's terrace house. The digging is continuing but the police refuse to comment. West will appear in court today. (→ 1/3)

NATO fires its first shots in anger over Bosnia

Belgrade, Monday 28
Four Serb warplanes which had severely damaged a Bosnian munitions factory at Novi Travnik with missiles were shot down today in NATO's first offensive action in its 45-year history. The Super Galeb light attack aircraft had twice ignored warnings to leave the UN's no-fly zone before American F16 fighters knocked them out of the sky with heat-seeking missiles. They stood no chance against the powerful F16s. One of the American pilots reported: "They were immediately destroyed and became fireballs. There were no parachutes." Two other Serb aircraft escaped. Admiral Jeremy Boorda, NATO commander in southern Europe, said the Serbs had twice ignored specific warnings. "We reacted exactly as we told them we would. If it was a test I think we passed the quiz." (→ 1/3)

USAF warplanes, flying from bases in eastern Italy, downed four Serb G-4 Super Galeb ground attack light aircraft.

Lillehammer Winter Games end in a

Jens Weissflog of Germany soars effortlessly through the frigid Arctic air to capture the ski jumping gold medal with a picture-perfect 133-metre-long jump.

Lillehammer, Sunday 27
The 1994 Winter Olympics games have come to an end. The warm welcome of the Norwegians and the icy beauty of the country helped make up for the disappointing British showing. Athletes from the UK are bringing home only two bronze medals – one of which was won by

the ice-dancing team of Jayne Torvill and Christopher Dean, whose performance many thought worthy of a greater recompense.

It is fitting that the big winner here is Norway. The Norwegians claimed the most medals, a total of 26, as they did when they hosted the 1952 Winter Games in Oslo. Their

hero was Johann Koss, the speed skater who set three world records, accounting for three of the 10 golds his country raked in. The favorite sport to watch among the home crowd was cross-country, which consistently drew huge crowds.

The Russians also made a fine showing, coming in third in the race

for the most medals, just one behind the Germans, who won 24. This score matched the showing of the Unified Team of former Soviet republics of which it was a part at the Albertville games of 1992. The Russians were thrilled to take the most golds, 11. The only big disappointment for the team was perhaps the

Not a good day for Tonya Harding.

Silver, not gold, for Nancy Kerrigan.

Gold and a new 1,500-metres world record for Norway's Johann Olav Koss.

spectacular blaze of glory in Norway

Unexpected champion: 26-year-old Diann Roffe-Steinrotter of New York State wins her first Super-Giant gold medal. It was her first win in nine years.

failure of their usually formidable hockey team to take home a medal.

The United States team won more medals here than they have in any other Winter Games. Skier Tommy Moe got the team off to a good start by taking the downhill gold on the very first day of competition. After a slip left speed skater Dan Jansen in eighth place in his specialty, the 500-metre race, he came back to set a world record and take the gold in the 1,000 metres. Unfortunately, the massive and intrusive press coverage of the tension between figure skaters Tonya Harding and Nancy Kerrigan somewhat overshadowed Kerrigan's winning the silver medal. Harding, under investigation in connection with the attack on Kerrigan, insists she had nothing to do with it. The US bobsledders were embarrassed to finish behind the Jamaican team. *Cool Runnings*, the film based on the Jamaicans' story, probably will not seem so funny to the US team now.

Many visitors to Lillehammer have proclaimed these Winter Games the best ever. They were certainly well run and popular with fans here and around the world. Some two million visitors, equal to nearly half the population of Norway, have come, and 88% of tickets offered were sold, the highest rate ever.

More hard-earned Nordic gold: Sweden defeats Canada in tense hockey final.

The sparkling closing ceremony. See you in Nagano (Japan) in 1998.

March

1994

Su	Mo	Tu	We	Th	Fr	Sa
		1	2	3	4	5
6	7	8	9	10	11	12
13	14	15	16	17	18	19
20	21	22	23	24	25	26
27	28	29	30	31		

New York, 1
A gunman opens fire on a van carrying Hasidic students, leaving one man brain dead and another critically wounded.

Gloucester, 1
Police find two more bodies in the garden of Frederick West; he is remanded in custody charged with the murder of his daughter. (→10)

St Vincent, 2
West Indies score 313 for six and England manage only 148 for nine in one-day cricket international.

London, 2
Foreign Secretary Douglas Hurd blames linkage of purchase of British defence equipment by Malaysia to investment in Pergau dam project on the former Defence Secretary Lord Younger.

London, 2
Mirror Group wins battle for the *Independent*; the paper's owners accept the group's £74.7 million offer.

North Korea, 3
UN begins inspections of North Korea's nuclear installations. (→23)

Bosnia, 4
Lieutenant General Rose calls for 5,000 more UN troops after a British base comes under mortar attacks two days in a row. (→18)

Rome, 4
Rock singer Kurt Cobain of Nirvana is hospitalised after overdosing on painkillers and champagne. (→8/4)

Beijing, 5
A week before a visit by US Secretary of State Warren Christopher, China's most prominent dissident, Wei Jingsheng, is detained for 30 hours, then released.

Dublin, 5
In the Five Nations rugby tournament, Ireland and Scotland tie 6-6. (→19)

Tel Aviv, 5
50,000 young Jews and Palestinians demonstrate for peace. (→31)

DEATH

4. John Candy, Canadian actor (*31/10/50).

Major wins Clinton's support for Northern Ireland peace efforts

The two leaders also discussed a joint scheme to rebuild shattered Sarajevo.

Washington, Tuesday 1
At the end of his two-day fence-mending visit to Washington, Prime Minister John Major won an endorsement from President Clinton today for his Northern Ireland peace initiative. The president, who has gone out of his way to be hospitable to Major, said: "I want to reaffirm the support of the United States for the joint declaration and for an end to the violence. I wish the prime minister and Mr Reynolds luck as they seek to carry this out." Neither man would be drawn about the controversial granting of a US visa to Sinn Fein chairman Gerry Adams. The prime minister insisted: "We didn't spend any time looking back over past problems." (→11)

Three new partners for European Union

Brussels, Tuesday 1
The European Community is set to expand from 12 members to 15 following the agreement of terms for Austria, Finland and Sweden to join on January 1, 1995. It took 36 hours of hard bargaining in continuous session before the deal was struck, with most difficulties stemming from Austria's reluctance to remove restrictions on foreign lorries using its Alpine passes. Eventually a face-saving compromise was reached. The agreement must now be ratified by the European parliament and by referendums in the three countries.

Muslims and Croats agree on federation

Washington, Tuesday 1
Under carrot-and-stick pressure from the USA, Bosnia's Croats and Muslims signed a peace agreement here today. The agreement unites Muslim and Croat territories under the Bosnian flag in a federation of Swiss-style cantons with a central government responsible for foreign affairs, trade and defence. There will be a two-house parliament and an annually rotating presidency. In a separate agreement the federation will form a loose economic union with Croatia. It will be boosted by US reconstruction aid. (→4)

Peace pact reached in Mexican rebellion

Mexico, Thursday 3
The Zapatista National Liberation Army, which launched an insurrection in January, has reached a peace pact with the Mexican government. The government has promised new rights and protections for Indian peasants in Chiapas state, new social programs and political, judicial and land reform. The government also proposed reform of the electoral system that has kept the ruling party in power for the last 65 years. The rebels will be allowed to keep their arms until the changes are carried out to their satisfaction. (→24)

March 1. Sting, best male pop singer at the Grammy Awards.

March 2. Supersonic Concorde reaches the ripe old age of 25: The French-assembled prototype, 001, first flew at Toulouse on March 2, 1969.

Torvill and Dean hang up their ice-skates

Their hour of glory, at the Copenhagen European championships in January.

Milton Keynes, Wednesday 2
Jayne Torvill and Christopher Dean announced their retirement from competitive ice dancing today at a fundraiser for the British Red Cross relief effort in the former Yugoslavia. They will not perform at the upcoming world championships in Japan but will embark on a final tour of professional demonstrations. The couple are satisfied by their recent performance at Lillehammer, though somewhat disappointed by coming in third in the Olympic competition. Dean called winning the bronze medal "bitter-sweet", saying: "We could not have skated any better than we did at the Games and would like to be remembered for that." Torvill added: "I think it was a good note for us to end on."

Four guilty verdicts in Trade Center plot

New York, Friday 4
In what Judge Kevin Duffy called a planned outburst, the four suspects in the case of the bombing of the World Trade Center screamed at the jury proclaiming their innocence after guilty verdicts were read.

The verdicts came just six days after the one-year anniversary of the bombing, which was a protest against US aid to Israel according to messages sent to news organizations by the plotters. Seven men have been charged in the attack; one is awaiting trial and two are still fugitives from the police.

Part-timers win vital Lords ruling on jobs

London, Thursday 3
Britain's part-time workers, most of whom are women, won a stunning victory today when the House of Lords ruled that the government discriminates against them and is in breach of European equality laws. The ruling by five law lords, with a majority of four to one, means that the government will have to extend unfair dismissal and redundancy rights to anyone with two years' service who works eight hours a week or more. More than five million Britons work part-time, almost a quarter of the workforce.

David Spedding to head UK spy service

London, Friday 4
Pursuing its new policy of semi-openness about the secret services, the government today named David Spedding as the next chief of MI6. A career intelligence officer and presently director of operations, Spedding, at 51, will be the youngest head of the Secret Intelligence Service, as it is officially known, since it was founded in 1909. He will succeed Sir Colin McColl, the first head of the service to be officially identified. One of his first tasks will be to move MI6 into its new £236 million headquarters at Vauxhall.

March 4. After the Batmobile, the Swatchmobile: Mercedes-Benz and Swatch present their tiny new bubble car, to be produced as from 1997.

March 4. In New York, Barbra Streisand's Art Deco objects fetch $5.8 million at Christie's. The star says she paid $135,000 for them in 1984.

March 5. The entente was not all cordiale, but England defeated France 18-14 in this Five Nations match, thanks largely to Rob Andrew's kicking.

Su	Mo	Tu	We	Th	Fr	Sa
		1	2	3	4	5
6	7	8	9	10	11	12
13	14	15	16	17	18	19
20	21	22	23	24	25	26
27	28	29	30	31		

Sindelfingen, Germany, 6
Colin Jackson sets world indoor record of 7.30 seconds in 60-metre hurdles. (→12)

Burundi, 7
More than 200, mostly Hutu, die in two days of massacres; residents blame killings on the Tutsi-dominated army.

Moldova, 7
In a referendum, 90% of voters reject union with Romania.

Moscow, 9
Former US President Nixon, who has visited Yeltsin's opponents on his trip to Russia, is snubbed by the president.

Kazakhstan, 10
President Nazarabayev's supporters win a clear majority in elections criticised as unfair by observers from the Conference on Security and Cooperation in Europe.

Kenya, 10
President Moi refuses to accept Richard Leakey's offer to resign as director of the country's conservation agency.

Santiago, 11
Eduardo Frei is sworn in as president in Chile's first peaceful handover of power since the inauguration of Salvador Allende in 1970.

Slovakia, 11
Vladimir Merciar's government falls as he loses a no-confidence vote in parliament.

Paris, 12
Colin Jackson wins 60-metre hurdles after prevailing in 60-metre dash yesterday in European Athletic Championships.

Indonesia, 12
President Suharto announces he will leave his post in 1998.

DEATHS

6. Max Schubert, producer of Australia's Grange Hermitage wine (*1915).

9. Fernando Rey, Spanish actor (*20/9/17).

9. Charles Bukowski, American poet and novelist (*16/8/20).

11. Evelyn Nightingale, British novelist (29/9/03).

11. Brenda Wootton, British folksinger (*10/2/28).

House of Horror man charged with the murder of eight women

Police say they may find more bodies in Frederick West's Gloucester house.

Gloucester, Thursday 10
Police charged a 52-year-old builder with the murders of eight women today in a case known as the "Nightmare on Cromwell Street". Police began digging in Frederick West's garden last month, looking for evidence in the disappearance of his daughter, Heather, last seen in 1987. They found a body, believed to be his daughter, and two others in the garden. More human remains were found buried in the cellar of the house and under a ground floor bathroom. Nine bodies have been unearthed so far. Police plan to widen their search to a field on the border with Herefordshire and to West's former Gloucester home. (→28/4)

March 6. Greek actress and politician, Melina Mercouri (*18/10/25), shown here in the 1960 film *Never on Sunday*, dies of lung cancer.

A dream comes true for women priests

Bristol, Saturday 12
The first women priests in the history of the Church of England were ordained in Bristol Cathedral today. Thirty-two women were ordained by the Bishop of Bristol, who spoke of the women's "significant journey." The two-hour service took on the atmosphere of rapturous celebration. As the "Amen" signalled the completion of their consecration, there were extraordinary scenes, with applause ringing round the cathedral's gothic arches and the new priests crying with joy.

March 9. The sporty star of the Geneva Motor Show: the V8-powered, computer-assisted Bentley Java coupé.

Pretoria moves in to stop homeland crisis

IRA launches new Heathrow mortar attack

Up to 60 people are reported to have been massacred in Bophuthatswana.

Rudimentary but very effective: the mortar tubes used to launch the bombs.

Bophuthatswana, Friday 11
This nominally independent "homeland" was torn by the chaos of rioting, looting and gun battles in the streets today. Lucas Mangope, the president of Bophuthatswana, has given in to the South African government's demands to drop his boycott of the upcoming elections, and Pretoria has sent in the South African Defence Force to restore order. When demonstrations against the boycott were joined by the homeland's own soldiers and police, Mangope said yes to an offer by white rightists to come in and defend him. Several thousand heavily armed members of the Afrikaaner Resistance Movement (AWB) began arriving yesterday, and today at least 12 and as many as 60 people have been killed in gun battles in the streets between the AWB, the homeland soldiers and protestors. (→ 28)

Heathrow, Friday 11
Four more IRA mortar bombs hit Heathrow just after midnight in the second attack in little more than 24 hours. Unlike the first mortars, fired from cars near the airport, this time tubes were set up on a trestle in nearby woodland. But fortunately, once again they failed to explode. Coded warnings had been received, and the airport was on full alert. The Queen, flying back from Bermuda, was told of the alert but instructed the pilot of her RAF VC10 to carry on with his intended flight path. She landed as the police were sweeping Terminal Four. The crump of the mortars, set off by a delayed-action mechanism, was heard some three hours later. Sinn Fein chairman Gerry Adams said in Dublin: "Every so often there will be something spectacular to remind the world the tragic signs of conflict are ongoing." (→ 13)

Loch Ness Monster was simply a wee submarine

London, Saturday 12
One of the best spiffing wheezes ever foisted on a gullible public is revealed today as a hoax. The world-famous picture of the Loch Ness Monster with its long head cruising serpent-like through the water, which has led to so many theories, books, films and tourist bawbies for the not-so-gullible Scots, was of a toy submarine bought for a few shillings and fitted with a head and neck made from plastic wood. The finished monster was a foot high and 18 inches long. The hoax was perpetrated by Marmaduke Wetherell, a self-styled big-game hunter and his two sons. Using Colonel Robert Wilson, a respected gynaecologist, as a front, they sold the picture to the *Daily Mail*. Now Christian Spurling, who helped build the monster, has spilt the beans.

March

1994

Su	Mo	Tu	We	Th	Fr	Sa
		1	2	3	4	5
6	7	8	9	10	11	12
13	14	15	16	17	18	19
20	21	22	23	24	25	26
27	28	29	30	31		

London, 13
Heathrow is shut down for two hours after a third IRA mortar attack in five days; Gatwick is also closed because of bomb threats. (→14)

New York, 13
In a television interview, Betty Shabazz, the widow of Malcolm X, says she believes Nation of Islam leader Louis Farrakhan was involved in the murder of her husband.

United States, 14
Apple launches its new computer, the Power Mac, based on a new micro-processor called the PowerPC.

Kenya, 14
US AC-130 warplane assigned to support forces in Somalia crash-lands offshore; one crewman was killed and 10 are missing. (→24)

London, 15
Prince Charles's Institute of Architecture launches the magazine *Perspectives*.

London, 15
Sir Charles Guthrie, a former SAS commander, succeeds Sir Peter Harding as Chief of the Defence Staff.

Portland, Oregon, 16
Tonya Harding enters a negotiated guilty plea to a charge of hindering prosecution in the case of the attack on Nancy Kerrigan; she will not go to jail but must resign from amateur skating as part of the agreement.

Alaska, 17
Martin Buser wins the 1,100-mile Iditarod Trail Sled Dog Race with a record time of 10 days, 13 hours, two minutes and 39 seconds.

Malaysia, 17
The RAF begins search for five soldiers missing on Borneo's Mt Kinabalu. (→25)

Cheltenham, 17
The Fellow wins jump-racing's most prestigious race, the Cheltenham Gold Cup.

Pailin, Cambodia, 19
Government forces seize Khmer Rouge headquarters.

DEATH

15. Mai Zetterling, Swedish actress and director (*24/5/25).

Scandal topples Sir Peter Harding, Britain's top military officer

London, Sunday 13
The Chief of the Defence Staff, Sir Peter Harding, resigned immediately today after a newspaper revealed his affair with Bienvenida Perez-Blanco, the divorced wife of former navy minister Sir Antony Buck. In a letter to Defence Secretary Malcolm Rifkind, Sir Peter, who is married and has four children, said he had not acted "in a manner that befits the holder of the post of Chief of the Defence Staff." There is much sympathy for Sir Peter, who, after their affair had ended and she had taken her story to the *News of the World*, was trapped into lunching with Bienvenida and was photographed kissing her goodbye. (→15)

Femme fatale? Bienvenida Buck revealed details of her affair with Sir Peter.

Bra companies fight battle of the bulge

Britain, Wednesday 16
Competition between Super-Uplift by Gossard and Wonderbra by Sara Lee Intimates, new underwired and slightly padded bras which aim to make women look a bit more like Claudia Schiffer, is shaping up nicely. The push-ups are seen on billboards and in magazines throughout the country. An advert showing a woman sporting not much more than the Wonderbra has just been declared "decent" by the Advertising Standards Authority. Super-Uplift is selling well here and in the USA; $18,000 worth were sold on its debut day in a New York store.

London and Dublin reject appeal by IRA

London, Monday 14
Sinn Fein chairman Gerry Adams's demand for Prime Minister Major to "clarify" last December's Downing Street declaration was rejected by both London and Dublin today. Irish Deputy Prime Minister Dick Spring said that unless there was "an absolute renunciation of the violence" there was no possibility of negotiations, and Downing Street officials reaffirmed there would be no negotiations with Sinn Fein until the IRA permanently ended its campaign of violence. (→17/4)

March 13. Sixteen seamen are killed in a fiery collision between a freighter and an oil tanker in the Bosphorus.

Prime Minister pays a surprise visit to Sarajevo

Sarajevo, Friday 18
In a lightning visit to Bosnia today, Prime Minister John Major flew by helicopter to visit the Coldstream Guards at Gornji Vakuf, met the men of the Duke of Wellington's at Bugojno and lunched in the mess hall at the British base in Vitez. He was then driven in General Rose's armoured Range Rover into Sarajevo to meet members of the Bosnian government and 200 citizens. Major announced a £12 million aid package for the city and indicated that more British troops might be sent to Bosnia as the country moves from war to peace. "We will do all we have to to monitor the peace," he said, "We must not let it slip." Today the Coldstream Guards band flies in for the reopening of the stadium with a football match between Sarajevo and the UN. (→ 20)

John Major, accompanied by Lieutenant-General Sir Michael Rose, tours the streets of the war-torn Bosnian capital.

Earth survives near-miss with an asteroid

Space, Tuesday 15
Earth just missed a catastrophic collision with an asteroid that would have caused an explosion equivalent to 20 nuclear bombs of the size that were dropped on Hiroshima. The asteroid passed about 100,000 miles from Earth – less than half the distance to the Moon and a near-hit on a cosmic scale. Two other such close shaves have been seen in the last three years. But Duncan Steel, who tracked the astral body at the Anglo-Australian Observatory near Sydney, says that "it's likely we're missing more than 99% of these things".

Clinton extends nuclear test moratorium

New Hampshire, Tuesday 15
As negotiations on an international nuclear test ban are being conducted in Geneva, the White House press secretary told reporters travelling with the president here that Bill Clinton had decided to extend the US moratorium on testing to September 1995. A Chinese test last October has not led to a resumption of testing by other nations, and the Clinton administration judged that restarting tests would harm the US objective of "securing the indefinite extension of the Nuclear Nonproliferation Treaty next year".

Despite defeat, Wales wins rugby championship

Twickenham, Saturday 19
The Queen watched the 100th match between England and Wales here today and was treated to a thrilling, skillful game which ended in victory and disappointment for both sides. The slide-ruler said that England, having suffered an unexpected defeat at the hands of the Irish, needed to win the game by 16 clear points in order to win the Five Nations Championship while Wales, outsiders at the beginning of the season, needed to beat England to win the ultimate prize, the Grand Slam. The tasks were beyond both sides. At one stage, when a rampant England were leading 15-3, it looked like they would snatch the championship, but in a final flourish Wales scored a vital try to make the final score 15-8. Wales lost the game but won the championship.

Su	Mo	Tu	We	Th	Fr	Sa
		1	2	3	4	5
6	7	8	9	10	11	12
13	14	15	16	17	18	19
20	21	22	23	24	25	26
27	28	29	30	31		

Tunis, 20
Opposition parties win seats in Tunisian parliament for the first time since independence from France in 1956.

Guyana, 22
England lose to West Indies by an innings and 44 runs; West Indies are now 2-0 up in the five-match cricket series.

London, 22
Lieutenant-General Michael Rose is knighted.

Washington, 22
Clinton lifts embargo on the sale of US military equipment to Estonia, Latvia, Lithuania, Albania, Romania and Bulgaria.

Siberia, 22
An Aeroflot A310 Airbus crashes, killing all 75 people aboard.

New York, 22
The US Federal Reserve raises short-term interest rates to 3.50%.

Malaysia, 23
Schindler's List is banned; censors call the film "Jewish propaganda". (→ 30)

North Korea, 23
Both North and South Korea are on military alert; Pyongyang refused to cooperate fully with inspections of nuclear sites by the International Atomic Energy Agency earlier this month and has threatened to pull out of the Nuclear Nonproliferation Treaty.

Nairobi, 24
Somalia's two main warlords sign peace pact. (→ 25)

Algeria, 25
The 200 British citizens living here are advised to leave by the Foreign Office; 32 foreigners have been killed in the country in the last six months.

DEATHS

22. Walter Lantz, American cartoon animator, creator of Woody Woodpecker (*1903).

23. Mgr Alvaro del Portillo, Spanish cleric, head of Opus Dei (*11/3/14).

24. Donald Swann, British comedy songwriter and performer (*30/9/23).

Clean sweep for Spielberg at Oscar Awards

As some celebrate, Britons bemoan their lack of recognition by Hollywood.

Hollywood, Monday 21
Steven Spielberg won his first Oscars, best picture and best director awards, for his film about the Holocaust, *Schindler's List*, in tonight's ceremony. Tom Hanks was named best actor for his portrayal of an attorney with AIDS in *Philadelphia*. Holly Hunter was best actress and 11-year-old Anna Paquin best supporting actress in Australian Jane Campion's *The Piano*. (→ 23)

Eric Cantona faces a severe sanction

Highbury, Tuesday 22
Fiery Eric Cantona, Manchester United's favourite Frenchman, was sent off for the second time in four days and inevitably faces a ban which could keep him off the field for three matches. His first dismissal, against Swindon Town, was for stamping on a prostrate opponent and last night, against Arsenal, for two bookable fouls. Both matches ended in two-all draws. Manchester, leading the Premier league, will be without Cantona's mercurial skills now at a crucial stage in the season, and there will be no "Oo! Ah! Cantona! " from the fans. (→ 10/4)

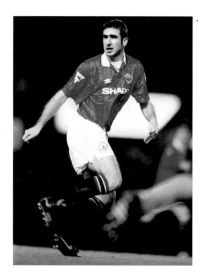

Visionary plan for global satellite network

Washington, Monday 21
The entrepreneurs behind Microsoft and McCaw Cellular Communications, the largest software and cellular phone companies, have taken the first steps in building a $9 billion satellite telecommunications system more ambitious than any seen before. Bill Gates and Craig McCaw have formed Teledisc Corp, a project which would send 840 satellites into close orbit of the Earth. The satellites would relay information ranging from telephone calls to high-resolution computerised images to the most remote parts of the globe.

March 20. Coldstream Guards parade in Sarajevo's Kosevo stadium at the start of a friendly match between the local team and an UNPROFOR squad. The peacekeepers lost four-nil, but a very good time was had by all. (→ 11/4)

Leading candidate for Mexico's presidency assassinated in public

The ruling party's man, Luis Donaldo Colosio, aged 44, lies dead in Tijuana.

Mexico City, Thursday 24
Mexico has been shaken by the assassination of Luis Donaldo Colosio, the ruling Institutional Revolutionary Party's (PRI) candidate to succeed President Salinas. The PRI has led Mexico for the last 65 years, and it was virtually certain that Colosio would have been the country's next president. The party leadership met this morning to discuss choices for a replacement candidate. The Mexican stock market, banks and currency exchanges are closed to prevent a financial crisis in the wake of the assassination. The government said that the suspected assassin, Mario Aburto Martinez, has confessed to yesterday's shooting in Tijuana.

Fellini's 'Juliet of the Spirits' is dead

Rome, Wednesday 23
Just five months after the death of her husband, Federico Fellini, Giulietta Masina (*22/2/20) has died of cancer. She starred in her husband's first film in 1951, *Luci del Varieta*, and the couple won international fame in 1954 when *La Strada*, in which she played an actress in a travelling theatre company, won an Oscar for the best foreign film. She was named best actress in Cannes for Fellini's 1957 film, *The Nights of Cabiria*. After much praise for *Juliet of the Spirits* in 1965, she did not make another film with her husband until *Ginger and Fred* in 1986.

American forces end operation in Somalia

Somalia, Friday 25
Today was E-Day, or Exit Day, for the remaining US troops in this East African country. A C25 Galaxy transport plane took off at 9:15am, followed by amphibious assault vehicles, which by noon had all left the airport, crossed the beach and headed into the sea. Before the departure, the Americans formally handed over control of the port and airfield to UN troops from Egypt and Pakistan.

Army team rescued after Borneo ordeal

Borneo, Friday 25
Two British army officers and three Hong Kong soldiers who had been missing for three weeks and were feared dead were rescued from the Borneo jungle today. Emaciated and exhausted, they were, according to their leader, Lt-Col Robert Neill, "down to our last two Polo mints". Other members of the 10-man expedition which split up while descending Mount Kinabalu emerged from the jungle two weeks ago.

Hillary gets a grip on First Kitchen

Washington, Saturday 26
Hillary Clinton has decided to wean her voracious pizza-loving husband away from junk food.

The First Lady hopes a move toward healthy all-American food will tempt Bill more than the French cuisine featured in the White House for years. Walter Scheib, the executive chef of the Greenbriar resort in Sulphur Springs, Virginia, has been picked to mastermind the menus for the Clinton family and their guests.

March 24. Regal headgear: The Queen admires the Imperial State Crown as she inaugurates the £10 million Jewel House at the Tower of London.

March 26. The Cambridge crew, boasting two German world champions, rows powerfully to a convincing victory in the 140th annual Boat Race.

March
1994

Su	Mo	Tu	We	Th	Fr	Sa
		1	2	3	4	5
6	7	8	9	10	11	12
13	14	15	16	17	18	19
20	21	22	23	24	25	26
27	28	29	30	31		

Wembley, 27
Aston Villa beat Manchester 3-1 to win the Coca-Cola Cup.

Turkey, 27
Premier Tansu Ciller's True Path Party comes in first in municipal elections, closely followed by the Islamic Welfare Party, which wins a surprise victory in Istanbul.

Leeds, 27
Tories of Yorkshire South West choose Christine Adamson as candidate for the European elections; the French woman is the first foreign candidate in a British Euro-election.

Manching, Germany, 27
Eurofighter 2000, designed and paid for by Britain, Germany, Italy and Spain, makes a successful first test flight.

Wolverhampton, 28
Graham Taylor, who resigned as manager of the national football team after the failure to qualify for the World Cup, becomes manager of the Wolverhampton Wanderers.

Middlesborough, 28
Masked man breaks into Hall Garth school and stabs to death one student and injures two others before teachers overpower him.

Paris, 29
In competition for the European Cup, Arsenal ties Paris-St-Germain 1-1.

Mexico City, 29
The Guatemalan government and four rebel groups sign a peace agreement.

Port of Spain, 30
West Indies now have unbeatable 3-0 lead in cricket series after beating England, who were bowled out for 46.

Malaysia, 30
The government agrees to allow screenings of *Schindler's List* if sex scenes are taken out; director Steven Spielberg refuses to cut out the scenes.

Israel, 31
Israel accepts stationing of international observers in Hebron as part of agreement to resume peace talks with PLO.

DEATH

28. Frances Donaldson, British author (*11/1/07).

Bullets fly in streets of Johannesburg

A gunfight erupts in the business district when ANC militants open fire on hundreds of armed Zulu demonstrators.

Johannesburg, Monday 28
Gun battles raged here today between Zulus and African National Congress supporters, and at least 18 people have been killed. But it was not just the violence that shocked South Africa. For the first time, the mayhem was centred in the most important city and the commercial heart of the country. Zulus marched in response to their King Goodwill Zwelithini's call for a boycott of next month's elections. Snipers opened fire on the marchers at Liberty Gardens, the main Zulu rallying point. Crowds of Zulus massed in front of two ANC offices and ANC guards opened fire on them, in self-defence they say. The two groups blamed each other for the bloodshed, adding that the police did nothing to head off the violence. (→ 8/4)

March 27. Michael Schumacher of Germany, in a Benetton-Ford, wins the Brazilian Grand Prix one lap ahead of Damon Hill's Williams-Renault.

Major's Euro-retreat infuriates many MPs

London, Tuesday 29
John Major's leadership came under savage attack today from his own party as well as the opposition over his retreat on European voting procedures. Rather than precipitate a full-scale European crisis, he has accepted the compromise worked out by Foreign Secretary Douglas Hurd in Greece; it concedes the principle that when four new states join the European Union next year, the number of votes needed to block EU legislation will rise from 23 out of 76 to 27 out of 90. This compromise weakens Britain's position and many MPs are furious about it. Maverick Tory Tony Marlow stunned the Commons by declaring Major had no credibility and should "make way for somebody else." The prime minister also faced trouble inside his cabinet where the Euro-sceptics were curbed only by the powerful alliance of Douglas Hurd, Kenneth Clarke and Michael Heseltine. An immediate revolt has been averted, but there is no doubt John Major is in trouble.

Right-wing media tycoon wins elections in Italy

Rome, Monday 28

Silvio Berlusconi, the right-wing media and soccer baron, has scored a remarkable success in Italy's general election. His Forza Italia (Onward Italy) party has won 155 seats out of 315 in the Senate, just three short of an absolute majority, and he is expected to pick up more votes with the Sud Tirol Volks Partij of the German-speaking minority. In the lower house, the right-wing alliance of the Northern League, Forza Italia and the neo-fascist National Alliance has a clear majority of 366 seats out of 630. These results are a stunning victory for Berlusconi, who only decided to enter politics in January "to stop the left". He based his new party on a network of 13,000 local clubs, a copy of his AC Milan's supporters clubs. The voters, disgusted with the corrupt old political parties, see him as a new broom. He has already laid claim to the premiership, but it may not be that easy. Rivalries are already surfacing in the alliance. (→ 10/5)

Some voters fear that Silvio Berlusconi's alliance with a neo-fascist party will bring renewed turmoil to their country.

Exit the Absurdist king, Eugene Ionesco

Paris, Monday 28

Eugene Ionesco, one of the foremost playwrights of the Theatre of the Absurd, died suddenly today at his home here in Montparnasse. Born in Romania on November 26, 1912, Ionesco was brought to Paris with his family shortly after his birth. He went back to his native country at 13 but returned to live in Paris all his adult life. His first play, *The Bald Soprano* (1950) was inspired by the nonsense he found in the language books he used to learn English. He continued to use the humour of that play, but his work also explored darker themes of power, death and despair in *The Lesson* (1951), *The Chairs* (1951) and *Exit the King* (1962).

Skull of earliest human ancestor is found

United States, Thursday 31

Scientists have found a fairly complete skull from humankind's earliest ancestors. The skull, found in the Ethiopian badlands, is from an *Australopithecus afarensis*, the same species as "Lucy", whose headless skeleton was found in 1974. The discoverers of the skull, whose work is revealed in today's issue of the magazine *Nature*, say that the skull proves that the human ancestors indentified as *afarensis*, who lived between 3 and 3.9 million years ago, are indeed a single species, not two as many scientists argue.

March. Barbie dolls, made by Mattel, are 35 years old this year and still going strong. In all, 700 million dolls have been sold worldwide since 1959.

April
1994

Su	Mo	Tu	We	Th	Fr	Sa
					1	2
3	4	5	6	7	8	9
10	11	12	13	14	15	16
17	18	19	20	21	22	23
24	25	26	27	28	29	30

Britain, 1
VAT on gas and electricity goes into effect.

Hungary, 1
Hungary becomes the first former Communist bloc nation to apply to join NATO's Partnership for Peace.

United States, 2
Authorities report that carjackings are increasing at an alarming rate.

Canterbury, 3
The Archbishop of Canterbury, Dr George Carey, says Tory policies are causing deep social divisions.

Luanda, 4
The Angolan capital is plunged into darkness as Unita rebels cut power lines supplying the city.

Iran, 4
Television satellite dishes are banned by the government.

London, 6
The Football Association cancels a friendly game due to be played in Berlin on April 20 because it coincides with Hitler's birthday.

Wales, 6
The governing body of the Church of Wales throws out a resolution allowing the ordination of women priests.

Rwanda, 7
Rioting breaks out in Kigali one day after the death in a plane crash of President Juvénal Habyarimana of Rwanda and President Cyprien Ntaryamira of Burundi. (→9)

Italy, 7
Lazio soccer star Paul Gascoigne fractures his leg during training.

Glasgow, 7
Scenes from a criminal trial are broadcast on television for the first time in Britain.

Liverpool, 9
Miinnehoma, owned by comedian Freddie Starr and ridden by Richard Dunwoody, wins the Grand National.

DEATHS

1. Robert Doisneau, French photographer (*14/4/12).

3. Frank Wells, president of Walt Disney (*14/4/12).

Round the world in 74 days for ENZA

Brest, France, Friday 1
Yachtsman Robin Knox-Johnston has smashed the non-stop round-the-world record by five days. He and his seven-man British and New Zealand crew brought their 92-foot catamaran *ENZA New Zealand* to the finishing line in 74 days, 22 hours, 17 minutes and 22 seconds. They faced atrocious weather in the last 24 hours and had to slow the boat to under 10 knots to ride the 50-foot waves thrown up by Atlantic storms. Co-skipper Peter Blake said what they feared most was nose-diving into the waves. One crew-member was thrown out of his bunk and landed in the galley. Welcomed by sirens and flares here tonight, Knox-Johnston said: "I'm looking forward to a pint of Guinness."

D-Day veterans win hotel skirmish against French bureaucrats

Paris, Monday 4
British and Canadian veterans won their second battle of D-Day today when they forced the embarrassed French government to promise that their long-reserved hôtel rooms in Normandy would not be taken away to make way for government guests and high-paying American television crews. Richard Duqué of the foreign ministry surrendered to their anger and said that all bookings made well in advance for the D-Day anniversary celebrations would be "honoured as planned. ... France wants to host and honour in the best conditions all those who fought for her liberation." (→21)

Suicide bomb attack kills nine in Israel

Afula, Israel, Wednesday 6
A car loaded with natural gas cannisters, nails and explosives burst into a metal-spewing fireball at a bus stop in this northern farm town, killing nine people, including the driver. Witnesses said victims were "burning like torches", and many of the 40 people wounded were treated for severe burns. Islamic militants claimed responsibility and said they were taking revenge for the massacre of Muslim worshippers at a mosque in Hebron. Israeli Foreign Minister Shimon Peres says that the attack will not stop negotiations on Palestinian self-rule.

April 8. Actress Diana Rigg's 'blazing intelligence' and 'elegant ferocity' are acclaimed by many New York theatre critics for her role as Medea.

Nirvana singer Kurt Cobain kills himself

Rwanda violence grows

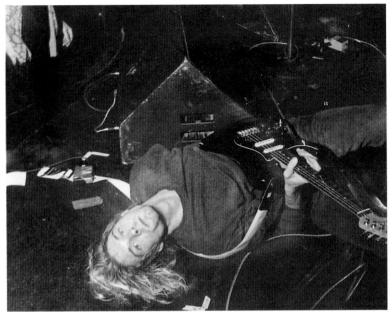

The 27-year-old grunge rock star was recovering from a drug overdose.

Belgian paratroopers are helping expatriate families escape from the carnage.

Seattle, Friday 8
"I Hate Myself and Want to Die" was the title Kurt Cobain had suggested for the latest album, *In Utero*, by his group Nirvana. Few are surprised, but many are saddened by the news that he was found dead today in his Seattle home; he had killed himself with a shotgun. Nirvana rose to the top of the charts in 1991 with their album *Nevermind*. It included the song "Smells Like Teen Spirit", which has become an ironic anthem for their fans, part of an age group that has been named Generation X. Cobain (*20/2/67) was seen as a new kind of rock star, but as his mother wept, referring to earlier rock deaths: "Now he's gone and joined that stupid club."

Kigali, Saturday 9
The streets of Kigali are littered with bodies as anarchy sweeps through the country in the aftermath of the death on Wednesday of President Habyarimana when his plane crashed – believed shot down. Bloody battles between the army, dominated by the majority Hutu tribe, and Tutsi rebels of the Patriotic Front have turned parts of the capital into no-go areas. Eleven Belgian UN soldiers were killed in one incident. Red Cross officials have reported up to 400 bodies in one hospital alone. Nuns, priests and aid workers are among the victims, and whole families are being slaughtered as neighbours turn on one another in a tribal killing frenzy. (→ 22)

'Son of Concorde'?

Paris, Thursday 7
The three largest European aerospace companies said today they would work together to develop technology for a bigger, faster successor to the Concorde. Tentatively called Alliance, the plane would have a range of 62,000 miles. This would allow it to reach Asia from Europe or the USA; the Concorde is limited to transatlantic flights.

Peace summit fails

Kruger National Park, Friday 8
The summit of South African political leaders called to persuade the Zulus to end their boycott of the nation's first multi-racial elections ended without agreement tonight. The best that the leaders, President de Klerk, Nelson Mandela, and Chief Buthelezi and King Goodwill of the Zulus, could do was to agree to continue negotiations. (→ 14)

April 8. Pope John Paul II celebrates Mass in the Sistine Chapel at the Vatican to mark the end of 14 years of painstaking restoration of Michelangelo's beautiful Judgement Day fresco, *Christ the Judge, and the Virgin*.

Britain, 10
Gad and Hans Rausing, the Swedish-born owners of TetraPak, topple the Queen from the top of the *Sunday Times* list of the richest people in Britain.

Argentina, 10
President Carlos Menem's Peronist Party wins parliamentary elections.

London, 10
Eric Cantona of Manchester United becomes the first foreigner to be voted soccer player of the year by the Professional Footballers Association.

Algiers, 11
Mokdad Sifi is appointed premier following the resignation of Redha Malek.

Moscow, 12
Russia and Belarus agree to unify their monetary systems and lift customs barriers.

Barbados, 13
England defeat the West Indies by 208 runs in the Fourth Test; it is the first time in 35 years that the West Indies have been defeated at home.

Johannesburg, 14
A mediation effort launched by Lord Carrington and Henry Kissinger to try to settle the dispute between Zulus and the ANC fails. (→ 24)

Washington, 14
US authorities approve the sale of female condoms.

Athens, 14
The parliament votes to strip former King Constantine and his family of their Greek citizenship and property.

Moscow, 15
Russia and Ukraine agree to divide the disputed Black Sea Fleet.

Britain, 15
A survey by the Institution of Environmental Health Officers reveals that rats outnumber the British population.

Bosnia, 16
A Royal Navy Sea Harrier is shot down by Serbs. (→ 17)

DEATH

10. Viktor Afanasyev, former editor of *Pravda* (*18/11/22).

NATO planes strike again at Serbs in bid to ease Gorazde's agony

Bosnians demonstrate in Sarajevo to call for stronger action to save Gorazde.

Sarajevo, Monday 11
NATO planes have attacked Serb positions around the beleaguered town of Gorazde for the second time in two days. The attack came after the Serbs shelled a school serving as a centre designated as a "safe-haven" for Muslim refugees. Two F18 Hornets of the US Marine Corps made the raid. They are reported to have destroyed a Serb tank and two armoured personnel carriers, and they returned safely despite heavy anti-aircraft fire. In Sunday's attack, two US F16 fighter-bombers were directed to their targets by SAS observers. The Serbs have reacted defiantly, accusing the UN and NATO of siding with the Muslims. They continue to shell Gorazde. A UN spokesman says that further air attacks could not be ruled out. (→ 16)

Key to cancer found

Washington, Monday 11
Scientists from the US National Institutes of Health said today that they have found the key to why cancer cells are virtually immortal. An enzyme produced by cancer cells reverses their normal ageing and dying process. The researchers say they could be two years away from developing a drug to block the enzyme. Such a drug would allow treatment to attack cancer cells directly and leave normal cells unharmed.

April 11. Wish you were here: Saucy postcards achieve respectability as Royal Mail stamps mark the centenary of the genre.

Government vows to fight video nasties

London, Tuesday 12
Home Secretary Michael Howard announced the toughest-ever crackdown on video nasties today, bowing to parliamentary and public pressure to bring in stringent controls to stop pornographic and sadistic films being seen by young children. The new measures will ban films such as *Child's Play 3*, linked to the James Bulger murder and the torture and murder of a young girl in Manchester, and *Juice*, linked to a murder in Cardiff where a man was kicked to death. Distributors and retailers who break the new laws will face strict punishments and may be sent to prison. The British Board of Film Classification will have to consider whether a video is "likely to cause psychological harm" to a child or likely to present "inappropriate role models" to children before granting a certificate. The ban will not apply to artistically important films containing violence.

April 11. Vladimir 'Mad Vlad' Zhirinovsky, Russia's ultranationalist politician, throws potted plants at Jewish demonstrators in Strasbourg, France.

Vital world trade treaty is signed at last

Representatives of more than 100 nations sign the 26,000-page document.

Marrakesh, Friday 15

To thunderous applause trade ministers from more than 100 countries signed the act embodying the Uruguay Round of the GATT negotiations here today.

The signing of the lengthy and complex document took four hours. It came to fruition after eight years of long and often bitter discussions and almost ended in disaster when the French threatened to block it in an obscure dispute about banana imports. The agreement is expected to increase world trade by £140 billion in 10 years.

Tobacco row grows in the United States

Washington, Thursday 14

Six chairmen from the biggest American cigarette companies appeared before Congress to deny claims by the Food and Drug Administration that they spike smokes with extra nicotine to keep their customers hooked. If the FDA decides that the companies do add nicotine, cigarettes could be prohibited like drugs such as cocaine or heroin.

USAF downs own copters

Iraq, Thursday 14

American F15s shot down two of their own helicopters this morning over the no-fly zone in northern Iraq, about 40 miles from the Turkish border. All 26 people on the two Black Hawks were killed. The passengers included 15 US military personnel, two British officers, a French officer, three Turkish officers and five Kurds.

It is not clear how the fatal mistake occurred. The pilots, hundreds of miles away from their base in southern Turkey, had the responsibility of deciding whether to attack. They flew in close to the craft in order to identify them but mistook them for the Soviet-built Hinds, with a different shape than the Black Hawks and about 6 feet longer, used by the Iraqis. Normally, a radio code would have indentified the helicopters as friendly. It is unknown if radio contact was attempted.

In Washington, President Clinton expressed his "deep sorrow at the tragedy" and said the full results of the Pentagon's investigation would be made public.

April 15. John Curry, OBE, (*9/9/49) former Olympic and world champion ice-skater, shown here at the 1976 Innsbruck Winter Games, dies.

April 14. Ravaged by fire last August, Lucerne's historic Pont de la Chapelle, dating from 1333, the oldest covered bridge in Europe, is reopened.

April 16. A three-dimensional view of Mammoth Mountain (top right), in California, based on radar images sent from the space shuttle *Endeavour*.

April
1994

Su	Mo	Tu	We	Th	Fr	Sa
					1	2
3	4	5	6	7	8	9
10	11	12	13	14	15	16
17	18	19	20	21	22	23
24	25	26	27	28	29	30

Bosnia, 17
Serb tanks enter the eastern town of Gorazde. (→ 24)

London, 17
Dionicio Ceron of Mexico wins the London Marathon.

United States, 17
The British film *Four Weddings and a Funeral* is number one at the box office, earning £2.8 million in two days.

London, 17
The musical *Sweeney Todd* and the drama *Machinal* carry off eight Olivier Awards.

London, 17
Irish Foreign Minister Dick Spring says that Dublin is prepared to make "constitutional sacrifices" for peace in Ulster. (→ 28)

Washington, 18
The Pentagon shelves its $8 billion Doomsday Project, a plan to keep the US government functioning after a major nuclear attack.

California, 19
Rodney King, the black motorist whose beating by white policemen led to the 1992 Los Angeles riots, is awarded damages of $3.8 million.

China, 20
The government rejects a British request for clemency for a jailed journalist, Xi Yang.

Berlin, 20
Authorities announce that Germans have replaced the French as the world's leading consumers of alcohol.

London, 21
The government climbs down in the face of protests by D-Day veterans that the 50th anniversary should be a commemoration rather than a celebration.

United States, 21
According to a survey, 65% of Americans do not know how many planets there are in the solar system.

London, 22
The Princess Royal is appointed Lady of the Most Noble Order of the Garter.

DEATH

20. Jean Carmet, French actor (*25/4/21).

Guildford Four man Paul Hill cleared of killing soldier in Belfast

The recent film In the Name of the Father *attracted attention to the case.*

Belfast, Thursday 21
Paul Hill, already released from prison as one of the Guildford Four, had another conviction quashed in the city's High Court today. Sir Brian Hutton, the Lord Chief Justice of Northern Ireland, told the court that Hill's conviction of the murder of Brian Shaw, a former British soldier, here in 1974 was "unsafe and unsatisfactory". Sir Brian said that "inhuman treatment" by policemen guarding Hill at Guildford police station, where he was being held over the IRA pub bombing, may have induced him to confess to the murder. Hill, who has married Courtney, one of the Kennedy family, can now take up American citizenship and claim up to £500,000 in compensation.

US troops train for warfare of the future in California desert

California, Thursday 21
Field test Operation Desert Hammer VI aims to point the way to the fighting of the future. The US Army is carrying out the test of high-tech equipment at a base in California. All armoured transports and personnel are fitted with radios, and their positions are sent via satellite, along with information gathered by planes, ground patrols and satellites, to computers. The computers will synthesize the data and create a display of the battle theatre which can be monitored by not only commanders at the rear but also the top brass at the Pentagon.

Batsman Brian Lara sets cricket record

St John's, Antigua, Monday 18
The West Indian left-handed batsman, Brian Lara, hooked English bowler Chris Lewis to the boundary just before lunch here today to pass Sir Garfield Sobers's record Test score of 365 not out, made in Jamaica 36 years ago. Lara, one of a Trinidad family of 11 children, is only 24, and the way he is batting he promises to break every record in the book. He was finally out today for 375. Sir Garfield was one of the first to congratulate him. He said: "I don't think a better batsman could have broken the record." (→ 6/6)

April 20. Barbra Streisand chose Wembley, where 10,000 fans gave her a standing ovation, to launch her first concert tour in more than 25 years.

Rwanda's killing fields are now drenched in blood

Kigali, Friday 22

The stench of death pervades the capital of Rwanda. Decomposing corpses are all around; the living have fled. The Red Cross estimated yesterday that more than 100,000 people have been killed in two weeks of slaughter, but nobody knows the real extent of the killing which has soaked every part of this lush and verdant land with blood. Now it is feared starvation and disease will sweep through the makeshift refugee camps. Even the small protection afforded by the UN force originally deployed to monitor peace accords between the government and Tutsi rebels will end when, as expected, the Security Council votes to withdraw the force. (→31/5)

Americans mourn Richard Nixon, their most controversial leader

New York, Friday 22

Richard Nixon (*9/1/13) was probably modern America's most controversial politician. His presidency came at a time when the country was divided, and Americans remain split in their views of the man. The Watergate scandal, which led to his resignation as president, caused many to see him as a devious, vengeful and even paranoid politician. But his foreign policy triumphs – especially the opening up of relations with China – have been widely praised, and in recent years he has taken a role of grey eminence to US presidents in this domain.

The only man to resign from the White House, shown with Henry Kissinger.

Frenchman gets life for wartime crimes

Versailles, Wednesday 20

Paul Touvier, member of the French militia in Lyons during World War II, today became the first Frenchman to be found guilty of crimes against humanity. Touvier, now 79, ordered the execution of seven Jews as a retaliation for the assassination of a Vichy minister by the Resistance, but he said he was ordered to execute 30 and managed to save 23 others. The prosecution presented evidence that he actively worked with the Gestapo. He was sentenced to life in prison.

70 Lost & Found

TERRIER LOST!!!

On Sunday in the Balloohbuie/Brig O' Dee area in the afternoon a tan and white terrier with long tail went missing. Any information or assistance that would lead to the return of this dog would be gratefully received.

Please ring either ▮▮▮▮ or Ballater Police Station.

A reward is being offered.

April 21. Prince Charles' Jack Russell, 'Pooh', is believed to have vanished down a rabbit hole.

US astronomers find dead star, planets

United States, Friday 22

In the current issue of *Science*, Alexander Wolszczan of Penn State University presents what he says is "irrefutable evidence" of a planetary system revolving around a star other than our Sun. His team found two planets turning around a pulsar, or dead star that emits invisible radiation instead of light, some 1,200 light-years away. The two planets, each about three times the mass of Earth, are unlikely to host any form of life. Their existence indicates that planetary systems may not be as rare as had previously been thought.

April 22. Michael Moorer, 26, becomes the first left-hander to win the world heavyweight title, after pounding Evander Holyfield in Las Vegas.

Su	Mo	Tu	We	Th	Fr	Sa
					1	2
3	4	5	6	7	8	9
10	11	12	13	14	15	16
17	18	19	20	21	22	23
24	25	26	27	28	29	30

Johannesburg, 24
A bomb blast kills nine people near ANC offices. (→ 29)

Bosnia, 24
Serb forces withdraw their heavy weapons from Gorazde. (→ 27)

London, 24
Schindler's List wins the British Academy of Film and Television Arts award for best film.

Oldham, 24
Wigan beat Oldham 50-6 to become Rugby League champions for the fifth consecutive season.

Seoul, 24
Jeremy Bates becomes the first British tennis player to win an ATP singles title in 17 years after beating Germany's Joern Renzenbrink.

Japan, 26
A China Airlines Airbus A300 crashes, killing all 262 people aboard.

Moscow, 27
President Boris Yeltsin accuses the CIA of stepping up its operations in Russia.

Bordeaux, 27
Graeme Obree of Scotland retakes the one-hour cycling record from Chris Boardman of England after covering 52.713 kilometres.

Gloucester, 28
Rosemary West, wife of the alleged serial killer Frederick West, is charged with jointly murdering three of the victims.

London, 28
The government accuses Iran of planning to provide the IRA with guns and funds. (→ 18/6)

Britain, 29
A poll shows that only 26% of voters support the Tories, the lowest level since they came to power 15 years ago.

DEATHS

25. David Langton, British actor (*16/4/12).

26. Queen Zein, Queen Mother of Jordan (*2/8/15).

27. Lynne Frederick, British actress (*24/7/54).

30. Richard Scarry, American author (*1919).

New Japanese premier already in trouble

Tsutomu Hata's shaky new government attempts to present a unified facade.

Tokyo, Monday 25
Tsutomu Hata became Japan's sixth prime minister in five years today and was immediately plunged deep into a political crisis when the Social Democratic Party, the biggest bloc in his coalition, walked out of his government on the grounds that it was too right-wing. Hata was elected to replace Morihiro Hosokawa, disgraced by shady financial dealings, but he is finding life at the top difficult. Mopping his forehead with a damp cloth today, Hata, a former bus company tour planner, said, "I am a man full of shortcomings."

Rightist candidate wins Salvador vote

San Salvador, Sunday 24
In the first peacetime elections in the country in 64 years, Armando Calderon of the rightist Republican Nationalist Alliance was elected president today. Only about half of the eligible voters came out to the polls on this rainy afternoon, but two-thirds of them cast their ballots for Calderon over Ruben Zamora, candidate of a leftist coalition.

UN forces to Bosnia as talks founder

New York, Wednesday 27
The United Nations approved the sending of 6,500 more troops to Bosnia today; there is, however, a marked reluctance on the part of member states to send their troops. The United States, for example, is willing to provide funds but will not commit its own forces, and there is no suggestion from the Ministry of Defence that it would add to the 3,350 British troops already there. Meanwhile the "Contact Group" of diplomats and experts from the US, Russia, the EU and the UN are due in Sarajevo to propose a cessation of hostilities and a partition of the country on ethnic lines. Its chances of success are nil. (→ 14/5)

Englishwomen seize rugby championship

Edinburgh, Sunday 24
The powerful England women's rugby union team beat the United States 38-23 in a splendid final here today to win the Women's World Cup. The game was one of contrasting styles, with the Americans delighting the crowd with the skill of their backs while the English relied, successfully, on their well-drilled pack to wear down their opponents.

Top quark, physicists' missing link, found after 20-year search

Batavia, Illinois, Tuesday 26
They had found charm and strange, up, down and bottom, but top, the sixth quark, remained elusive. Scientists here at the Fermi National Accelerator Laboratory today presented evidence of the top quark.

Quarks, along with leptons, are the building blocks of atoms. The evidence for the top quark, if confirmed, will complete the experimental proof of the Standard Model of theoretical physics, which for the last two decades has been accepted as the most viable theory to describe the atom and its structure. To hunt quarks, scientists conduct expensive experiments in which particles, accelerated to the speed of light, are crashed together. The resulting explosions yield clues about these smallest building blocks of matter.

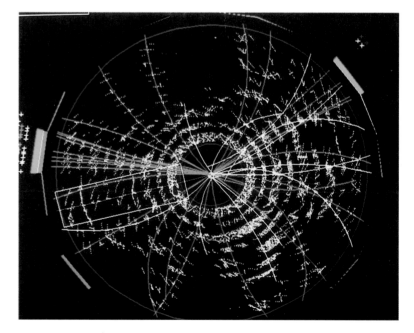

South Africa sees dawn of freedom in historic vote

Black residents of a township near Johannesburg are prepared to queue for hours to cast their ballots in the nation's first-ever truly democratic elections.

Johannesburg, Friday 29
Nelson Mandela, the 75-year-old president of the African National Congress, is heading for a resounding victory in South Africa's historic first all-race elections. Despite initial fears of right-wing violence and organizational problems on the first day of voting which left many polling stations without ballot papers, the election is being hailed by all parties as being free and fair. Dissolving the old apartheid government, President de Klerk said: "The long and frustrating years of negotiation, the drama of confrontation and conflict are all preludes to the great test that lies ahead: The challenge that a new democracy will take root and flourish in our country."

The people have responded to this challenge in a moving and dignified display of enthusiasm for their first exercise in democracy. On the first day of voting, hundreds of thousands of sick, elderly and handicapped, determined to cast their votes, walked, hobbled or were carried to the polling booths. Mandela, triumphant but modest, spoke tonight of his "joy, hope and confidence for the future". (→ 10/5)

April 26. The British Library pays £1 million for the only known complete version of the New Testament translated by William Tyndale in 1526.

CIA's masterspy Ames gets a life sentence

Alexandria, Virginia, Thursday 28
Aldrich Hazen Ames, who pleaded guilty to charges of spying against the US for the KGB, told the judge who sentenced him to life in prison that he had worked for the Russians because the CIA had become a "self-serving sham" that fooled the government into believing their work was valuable and because of "a shift to the extreme right in our political spectrum". He also pleaded guilty to evading taxes on the money paid him by the Soviet Union, now said to have totalled more than $2.5 million. His wife Rosario also pleaded guilty to tax evasion and spying. She is to be sentenced later and faces five to six years in prison.

Su	Mo	Tu	We	Th	Fr	Sa
1	2	3	4	5	6	7
8	9	10	11	12	13	14
15	16	17	18	19	20	21
22	23	24	25	26	27	28
29	30	31				

Dublin, 1
Ireland wins the Eurovision song contest for the third successive year.

Cuba, 1
President Fidel Castro gets the parliament's go-ahead to enact far-reaching economic reforms.

France, 1
Welsh golfer Ian Woosnam wins the Cannes Open.

Sheffield, 2
Stephen Hendry wins the Embassy World Snooker title.

Cairo, 3
Five Muslim militants are executed for attempting to kill premier Atef Sedki last year.

China, 3
The government admits that there is a serious breakdown of authority in rural regions.

Copenhagen, 4
Arsenal beat Parma 1-0 to win the European Cup Winner's Cup.

London, 4
Prince Charles says the fashion of political correctness is destroying much of the fabric of British society.

Singapore, 5
An American teenager, Michael Fay, receives four strokes of a cane for vandalism.

Abidjan, 5
In a bid to ease unemployment and raise tourist revenue, the Ivory Coast decides to lift a 20-year-old ban on big game hunting.

Vietnam, 6
The government celebrates the 40th anniversary of the battle of Dien Bien Phu, which ended French colonial rule.

Southampton, 7
Yachtsman Mike Golding shatters the record for circumnavigating the world from east to west, taking just 167 days.

Washington, 7
President Clinton denies charges of sexual harassment made by Paula Jones, a former Arkansas state employee.

DEATH

7. Aharon Yariv, former head of Israel's Military Intelligence (*20/12/1920).

Formula One super-champ Ayrton Senna dies in high-speed crash

Imola, Italy, Sunday 1
Ayrton Senna, winner of 41 Grand Prix and foremost Formula 1 driver, died today after spinning off a curve at the San Marino Grand Prix and hitting a concrete wall. Yesterday, Austrian Roland Ratzenberger met his death at nearly the same spot during a qualifying run. This was the third GP to be held since active suspension and automatic driving aids were banned in order to make F1 more of a "drivers' championship". Former F1 stars and current pilots are calling for the creation of a drivers union to promote safety in the sport. Sadly and ironically, former champion Niki Lauda had named someone who could organize such a group just before today's race: "It needs a strong personality to take care of this, and at the moment I think this is Senna."

The 34-year-old Brazilian driver died shortly after hitting a wall at 150mph.

Israel, PLO sign pact ending the occupation of Gaza and Jericho

The historic ceremony in Cairo came after six months of tough negotiations.

Cairo, Wednesday 4
Israel and the PLO concluded a long-awaited agreement on Israel's withdrawal from the Gaza Strip and Jericho here today – but only after a last minute hitch nearly wrecked the ceremony. Yasser Arafat signed the text of the 200-page agreement but, stony-faced, refused to sign the accompanying maps. There was confusion among the dignitaries on the stage, an adjournment was called and another compromise made: Arafat would sign the map in exchange for an Israeli letter confirming that doing so did not constitute agreement to the borders. (→ 13)

Poll disaster for Tories

London, Thursday 5
The Conservative Party has suffered a shattering defeat in local elections, losing 429 council seats and control of 18 councils. The Tories have been ousted from power in their traditional heartlands in the south of England, and senior Tories say the result is the worst possible precursor for the European elections in June.

Standing on the steps of No 10 Downing Street – from which many believe he will soon be ousted – John Major conceded that his party's losses were the result of national rather than local discontent. The "deep bruises" caused by the recession and disunity in the party resulted in many Tory supporters staying at home. But, he said, there was no point in "whingeing", and he called on the party to unite behind him to fight the Euro-election.

Leaders of the other parties are jubilant. Labour's John Smith anticipates victory in an early general election. The Liberal Democrats' Paddy Ashdown declared: "We are no longer the third party, but one of the three parties." (→ 13/6)

May 5. Hugh Hefner, 68, marks *Playboy*'s 40th anniversary.

The Queen, Mitterrand inaugurate Channel Tunnel

Coquelles, Friday 6

Two centuries of dreams and eight years of struggle became reality today when Queen Elizabeth and President Mitterrand cut red, white and blue ribbons to open the Channel Tunnel. The Queen, having first opened the Eurostar passenger terminal at Waterloo, passed through the tunnel to Coquelles, where the trains of the two heads of state met nose to nose. After the ceremony and spirited renditions of the national anthems by the Garde Republicaine, there was time for lunch, and then the Queen and the president sat in the royal Rolls Royce as it was carried back to England on Le Shuttle for another opening ceremony. The tunnel was, said the Queen, a mixture of French elan and British pragmatism.

US Congress finally approves Clinton's gun control programme

America's powerful gun lobby fought tooth and nail against the weapons ban.

Washington, Thursday 5

A 216-214 vote in the House of Representatives has approved a ban on assault weapons. President Clinton had the support of police organizations and of former presidents Ford, Carter and Reagan for the Bill. But the National Rifle Association condemned it as contrary to the constitutional right to bear arms. A similar Bill was rejected in 1991, and as late as this morning, defeat was expected. One representative who changed his mind to vote for the ban said: "The right to bear arms does not give an American citizen the right to park a howitzer in his garage."

Bannister's record run is remembered

Oxford, Saturday 7

Forty years ago a young medical student named Roger Bannister broke the 4-minute-mile barrier, a feat once thought impossible. Today, at the same Iffley Road track, some of the world's finest runners met for a handicap race at the end of a week of celebrations in honour of Bannister, now Sir Roger. Kip Keino of Kenya, still fit at 54, won the race. "It was", he said, "an honour just to run where he broke the record." Bannister thought it was the perfect end to a perfect week.

May 6. Viscount Linley launches his £10,000 wooden cigar boxes.

Franglais fanatics will now face fines

Paris, Thursday 5

No English, please, we're French.

The National Assembly has approved a Bill to ban public use of foreign (that is, English) words. Critics say the ban is unenforceable and gives a nationalist and defensive image to the country. Scientists fear their influence will be limited if they have to stick to French for publications and conferences. Fines of up to 20,000 francs (£2,300) would be imposed for using a foreign word when a French one will do. (→ 5/7)

May 6. The rising cost of true love: Richard Gere and Cindy Crawford pay £20,000 for an advert in *The Times* to say they are happily married.

May

1994

Su	Mo	Tu	We	Th	Fr	Sa
1	2	3	4	5	6	7
8	9	10	11	12	13	14
15	16	17	18	19	20	21
22	23	24	25	26	27	28
29	30	31				

St Mellion, Cornwall, 8
Golfer Seve Ballesteros wins the Benson and Hedges International Open.

Algiers, 8
Suspected Muslim extremists kill two French priests.

Milan, 8
Canada wins the World Ice Hockey Championship.

Panama, 9
Ernesto Balladares, a banker and former minister, wins the presidential elections.

Normandy, 9
The new Pegasus Bridge over the canal at Benouville, the first site liberated by British troops on D-Day, opens to traffic.

London, 10
John Major rules out a referendum on closer EU ties.

Westminster, 10
MPs vote to lift restrictions on High Street betting shops.

Rome, 10
Prime Minister Silvio Berlusconi's new government includes five ministers belonging to the neo-fascist National Alliance.

Chicago, 10
John Wayne Gacy, one of America's most notorious serial killers, is executed for the murder of 33 boys.

Milan, 11
Inter Milan wins the UEFA Cup after beating Casino Salzburg of Austria 1-0.

Frankfurt, 11
The Bundesbank cuts interest rates to their lowest levels in five years.

Washington, 12
Congress approves a controversial Bill banning violence, blockades and threats against abortion clinics.

Athens, 13
Following violent protests from young Greeks, the government drops a law requiring all nightclubs to close by 2am.

DEATHS

8. Lady Victoria Wemyss (*27/2/1890), last surviving godchild of Queen Victoria.

12. Roy Plunkett, inventor of Teflon (*1911).

President Nelson Mandela takes oath

The former prisoner, South Africa's first black head of state, shakes hands with his predecessor, Frederik W de Klerk.

Pretoria, Tuesday 10
Nelson Mandela, who spent 27 years in jail as a prisoner of the apartheid regime, was inaugurated today as South Africa's first black president. The ceremony, held in baking sunshine, was attended by the largest assembly of foreign dignitaries ever seen in Africa. The Duke of Edinburgh, wearing a panama hat, represented the Queen. Hillary Clinton, Benazir Bhutto, Fidel Castro and Yasser Arafat were among the VIPs who heard Mandela vow that never again would South Africa be "the skunk of the world". The day, however, belonged to the tens of thousands of ordinary South Africans who, in emotional scenes of jubilation and racial harmony, danced and sang on the lawn outside the Union Buildings. After taking the oath, the new president said he knew there was no easy road to freedom, but he urged the cheering crowd: "Let there be justice for all. Let there be peace for all. Let there be work, bread, water and salt for all." He continued: "The time for the healing of the wounds has come, the moment to bridge the chasms that divide us has come, the time to build is upon us." And he praised his predecessor, F W de Klerk, the man who freed him from prison and is now one of his two deputy presidents, for his historic vision. He hailed De Klerk as one of the "greatest sons of Africa" and urged the people to foster the spirit of forgiveness. Speaking in Afrikaans, he said, "What is past, is past." (→ 25)

May 8. Hero of *A-Team*, George Peppard (left) (*1/10/1928), dies.

Haiti's military rulers defy United Nations

Port-au-Prince, Wednesday 11
Despite the condemnation by the United Nations of the junta that ousted Haiti's elected President Jean-Bertrand Aristide and the economic embargo against the country, a group of legislators today installed Emile Jonassaint, a Supreme Court judge, as "provisional president" in the presence of army commander General Raoul Cédras, the strongman who holds real power in the country. The move is seen as an attempt to consolidate the military government's power and was denounced by the White House as "cynical, unconstitutional and illegal". Many US legislators are now pushing for military intervention to restore Aristide. (→ 22)

Father Aristide, president-in-exile.

Britain stunned by sudden death of Labour leader

London, Thursday 12

John Smith, the Labour leader who was both popular and respected, died this morning after his second heart attack. He was 55. As news of his death spread through Westminster, MPs gathered at the House to pay their respects to a man who stood every chance of becoming the first Labour Prime Minister since 1979. Like Hugh Gaitskell and R A Butler, he will be numbered among the best prime ministers the country never had. Taking over from Neil Kinnock, he had raised his party's hopes from deep depression to a genuine expectation of victory. John Major paid tribute to him: "I think of him as an opponent, not an enemy, and when I remember him I shall do so with respect and affection." The sorrow was not confined to Westminster; the whole nation mourns a good man. (→21)

Jericho cheers police

Jericho, Friday 13

Crowds danced, beat drums and waved the Palestinian flag today as some 460 Palestinian police rode into town to take over the army base and police station that had been the Israeli headquarters here. So far, the Palestinians have assumed control of about half of the territory they will run under the self-government agreement with Israel.

Manchester win cup

Wembley, Saturday 14

Manchester United beat Chelsea 4-0 today to win the FA Cup in a match in which Chelsea, who have beaten Manchester twice this season, dominated the first half and might well have won; but they did not seize their chances. Manchester, after a year in which they have dominated English football, have now won the Cup and the League championship.

Bosnia's president rejects new truce plan

A clearly dejected Lord Owen leaves Geneva after the latest round of talks.

Sarajevo, Saturday 14

Hopes for peace in Bosnia received another setback today. President Izetbegovic rejected a call by the US, Russia and five EU states for a four-month ceasefire and negotiations on a division of territory in which Bosnian Serbs would control 49% and the Croat-Muslim federation 51%. The Croats and Muslims have reverted to their initial demand for control of 58% of the proposed mini-state, and Izetbegovic is insisting on a truce of only two months. He is fearful that the Serbs, who control 70% of Bosnia and are arguing for an indefinite truce, would use a long ceasefire to carry out more "ethnic cleansing" to consolidate their military gains. (→9/6)

May 12. The world's tallest rollercoaster, on which screaming passengers hurtle down a record 65 degree incline at 85mph, is unveiled at Blackpool.

Su	Mo	Tu	We	Th	Fr	Sa
1	2	3	4	5	6	7
8	9	10	11	12	13	14
15	16	17	18	19	20	21
22	23	24	25	26	27	28
29	30	31				

Moscow, 16
Armenia and Azerbaijan agree to a ceasefire in the disputed enclave of Nagorno-Karabakh.

Vienna, 16
Salman Rushdie is presented with Austria's prize for European literature.

Dominican Republic, 17
President Joaquin Balaguer is elected for a third term.

London, 17
President Robert Mugabe of Zimbabwe begins his first state visit to Britain since his country's independence in 1980.

Athens, 18
AC Milan win the European Champions' Cup, beating FC Barcelona 4-0.

Washington, 18
The Food and Drug Administration approves the sale of the first genetically engineered tomato.

London, 19
A first edition of *The Tale of Peter Rabbit* is sold for a record £63,250.

Newcastle, 19
Robert Black, a former van driver, is given 10 life sentences for abducting and murdering three schoolgirls.

Turkey, 19
Kurdish militants say they will step up attacks on tourist sites.

Hong Kong, 20
Talks between Britain and China on the financing of Hong Kong's new airport fail.

Scotland, 21
Labour leader John Smith is buried in Reilig Odhrain, the ancient royal burial place of Scottish and Norse kings, on Iona.

Britain, 21
Mary Whitehouse, aged 83, steps down as president of the National Viewers And Listeners Association.

DEATHS

15. Duncan Hamilton, British racing driver (*30/4/20).

15. Gilbert Roland, American actor (*11/12/05).

19. Luis Ocana, former Spanish cycling champion (*9/6/45).

Jackie, the Queen of Camelot, is dead

New York, Thursday 19
Jacqueline Kennedy Onassis, born in Southampton, Long Island, on July 28, 1929, was loved and admired by Americans and around the world. Her beauty and sophistication helped create the Camelot myth of her husband's presidency. When John Kennedy died, her courage was lauded, and she gave strength to a nation in mourning. Her later marriage to an older Greek shipping tycoon, Aristotle Onassis, at first caused some controversy in the States. For many, she would always be Jackie Kennedy, but for others, she became a symbol of international high society – Jackie O. For the last few years, she epitomised the successful businesswoman as a top-level editor. Her struggle against cancer was revealed earlier this year; she died today at the age of 64.

President John Kennedy and Jacqueline at Buckingham Palace in June 1961.

Prince of Wales pays tribute to victims of the siege of Leningrad

Prince Charles is shown around the Cathedral of the Peter and Paul Fortress.

St Petersburg, Tuesday 17
Prince Charles laid a wreath today at the bronze statue of Mother Russia which commemorates the one million people who died from starvation and enemy action during the heroic 872-day defence of the city against the German besiegers. In the faded splendour of the Hermitage theatre in the old Winter Palace, he told a group of Russian and British businessmen that he hoped Britain and Russia could return to the spirit of warm cooperation of pre-Soviet Union times. "The British people", he said, "never had any quarrel with the Russian people."

Earliest European is found in England

Boxgrove, Sussex, Tuesday 17
A section of legbone, found in a gravel pit here last year has proved to come from "the earliest European", who lived 500,000 years ago. Named "Boxgrove Man", he was a six-foot prehistoric heavyweight who scavenged and hunted, using hand axes. Announcing these findings today, Dr Geoffrey Wainright, chief archaeologist for English Heritage, said, "We are reaching back to the very origins of mankind."

May 15. Michael Schumacher wins the Monaco Grand Prix today, three days after Austria's Karl Wendlinger (above) was injured during practice.

Malawi's new leader, Muluzi, takes office

Blantyre, Saturday 21

The 30-year dictatorship of Dr Hastings Banda as ruler of Malawi has been ended by the first free election in this poverty-stricken country. The ailing despot, now 95, was soundly defeated in an election he would never have permitted in his prime.

The victor, who took office as president today, is Bakili Muluzi, 51, a former supporter of Banda. One of the few politicians who deserted Banda's Malawi Congress Party and lived, the new president ran an underground network working for democracy. The changes that led to the free election were eventually forced on Banda by foreign aid donors. Muluzi has no doubt about his priorities: "My village has no clinic, no school, bad roads. People walk without shoes."

Northern Yemen forces advance on Aden as secession proclaimed

Forces loyal to South Yemen's leader, Ali Salem Baid, are set to defend Aden.

Aden, Saturday 21

Just hours after declaring itself an independent state, thus dissolving a union only four years old, south Yemen seems headed for disaster as the stronger, better-equipped northern army advances on the capital. The base guarding the approaches has already fallen, and there is little to stop the northerners except exhaustion and logistic problems.

The seeds of the civil war which is tearing apart the only democratic republic on the Arabian peninsula stem from the secular and formerly Marxist south's fears that it is being marginalised by the conservative, tribal north. Oil is involved, with the impoverished south suspecting that the north was using the union to grab new oil discoveries on southern territory. This, combined with Saudi religious meddling, is an explosive mixture. (→ 6/6)

Police to have guns and US-style batons

Brighton, Wednesday 18

The British bobby's wooden truncheon is to be replaced by the US-style side-handled baton. Home Secretary Michael Howard told the Police Confederation here today that tests had shown the batons to be effective in warding off violent criminals and merely drawing the batons had a pacifying effect. Howard also told the conference that while the government remained opposed to the general arming of police, more officers on armed response vehicles would openly wear sidearms.

'Missing' Van Gogh paintings revealed during X-ray examination

Amsterdam, May

Recent X-ray examinations of all the works that Vincent Van Gogh painted in the Netherlands, Antwerp and Paris have revealed others that have been unknown previously or thought lost. Van Gogh often cut up or painted over canvases. Art experts at the Van Gogh Museum here hypothesize that he did so because he felt them unsuccessful. Though very critical of his own work, he was attached to the paintings he esteemed. Pictured here is *Self-portrait with pipe and glass*: The X-ray photo reveals another portrait of a bare-breasted woman.

Tennis star Capriati is caught with drugs

Coral Gables, Florida, Monday 16

Jennifer Capriati, the troubled tennis star who turned pro at the age of 13, was arrested today on charges of possession of marijuana. Police searched her hotel room after receiving a tip that a 17-year-old runaway girl was staying there. They found the drugs in her knapsack. Capriati, who is now 18 and has temporarily stopped playing tennis, had been arrested for shoplifting in Florida last December.

May 19. As part of a summer-long series of sumo-inspired events in central London, two 12-foot-tall latex wrestlers took to the streets of the City today.

Details of Churchill death plot revealed

London, Friday 20

Wartime documents released today show that the German secret service recruited Islamic fundamentalists to kill Winston Churchill while he was visiting the Middle East in 1941. The plot was discovered by Britain's code-breakers at Bletchley Park, and Churchill was warned that "attempts are going to be made to bump you off". He took note of the warning, cancelled a visit to Algiers and went home.

May

1994

Su	Mo	Tu	We	Th	Fr	Sa
1	2	3	4	5	6	7
8	9	10	11	12	13	14
15	16	17	18	19	20	21
22	23	24	25	26	27	28
29	30	31				

Germany, 23
Roman Herzog is chosen to replace Richard von Weizsäcker as president.

Mecca, 23
More than 255 Muslim worshippers are killed when crowds surge toward a sacred cavern.

London, 23
The 81st Chelsea Flower Show opens amid controversy after some exhibitors said they had bought plants from Holland to stock their stands.

Australia, 24
Four people are killed when a car taking part in the 3,800-kilometre Cannonball Run race across the Northern Territory crashes.

Geneva, 24
The World Health Organization reports that Japanese women have the longest life expectancy in the world, 83 years.

Brussels, 24
Russian Defence Minister Pavel Grachev says his country will join NATO's Partnership for Peace. (→ 22/6)

London, 25
The government chooses Camelot Group to run the National Lottery.

France, 25
A football manager is given a six-month suspended sentence for putting valium into an opposing team's water bottles at half time.

New York, 25
The UN lifts the arms embargo on South Africa. (→ 20/7)

Washington, 26
President Clinton ends the linkage between human rights and US trade with China.

Barcelona, 29
Damon Hill wins the Spanish Grand Prix.

DEATHS

24. John Wain, British novelist, poet and critic (*14/3/25).

29. Erich Honecker, former East German president (*25/8/12).

30. Baron Marcel Bich, inventor of the Bic ball-point pen (*29/7/14).

Haitians face international embargo

As sanctions begin to bite, day-to-day life will be even tougher for Haitians.

Haiti, Sunday 22
Tougher sanctions meant to force the military from power in Haiti go into effect today. No exports will leave the country, and only basic foodstuffs, medicine and cooking fuel will be allowed in. But hopes are not high that the sanctions will work. Last week, US President Bill Clinton said he was seriously considering using military force against Raoul Cédras's junta. He said that the US had a strong interest in re-establishing democracy in its "back-yard" and stressed the threat of a "massive outflow" of refugees if the military remained in power. The new sanctions are likely to increase the numbers of Haitians headed for Florida in their rickety craft. (→ 3/6)

'Galloping gangrene' outbreak causes growing concern in Britain

London, Tuesday 24
A killer bug that destroys tissue and muscle is believed to have claimed a sixth victim. "Galloping gangrene" literally eats away at its victims so that they die within a few hours. Public concern is growing and the Department of Health has given hospitals and health laboratories details of the infection. However, doctors are pointing out that the bug, a streptococcal strain, is nothing new and that only rarely does it turn deadly. Dr Robin Stott says: "We must put this in perspective and not cause alarm."

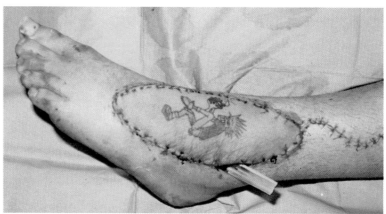

Some victims of the tissue-destroying bacterial infection are saved by grafts.

Tarantino's 'Pulp' wins Cannes award

Cannes, Monday 23
The announcement by Cannes jury president Clint Eastwood that the violent and black-humoured *Pulp Fiction* had won the Golden Palm was met by cheers and jeers. Surrounded by cast members Bruce Willis, John Travolta and Samuel Jackson, 31-year-old director Quentin Tarantino made an obscene gesture at one of his hecklers and noted: "I don't make movies that bring people together. I make movies that split people apart." Though he has his detractors, most critics are united in praising the young video-store clerk turned Hollywood *wunderkind*.

May 24. Reminiscent of the legendary Testarossa, Ferrari's new V8-powered 355, a lighter 380hp version of the 348, is presented to the public.

Russia's most famous exile returns at last

Alexander Solzhenitsyn in Magadan, in the heart of the Gulag Archipelago.

Vladivostok, Friday 27
Alexander Solzhenitsyn, author in the great Russian tradition and survivor of the war, cancer and Stalin's death camps, came home today after 20 years of exile in America. He went first to Magadan, the port of the Gulag Archipelago, where he paid tribute to Stalin's victims. Later, he told thousands gathered to greet him he never doubted communism was doomed. He said: "I know I am arriving in a Russia tormented, disheartened, in shock, changed beyond recognition and still searching for itself and for its own meaning."

Rwanda's death toll estimated at 500,000

Foreign and local aid workers can no longer cope with the ghastly situation.

Rwanda, Tuesday 31
The terror continues in Rwanda. Unconfirmed reports tell of a massacre of 500 people Saturday in a camp 30 miles south of Kigali. Aid organizations say the death toll has reached 500,000, and 1.5 million people are homeless. Hutu radio station RTLM yesterday continued to incite killings of Tutsi in its broadcasts. The 450-man UN force that was evacuating people from Kigali temporarily stopped operations today after a Senegalese captain was killed by mortar fire that hit his vehicle. (→ 2/6)

Beggars are 'offensive' says John Major

London, Friday 27
John Major described beggars as eyesores tonight and called for "rigorous penalties" to be applied to remove their "offensive and unjustified" presence from the streets. His remarks, in an interview in Bristol's *Evening Post* have set off a fierce political controversy, with the opposition and charity organizations accusing him of "picking on the powerless". The prime minister argues that the benefit system means there is no need for anyone to beg.

Slanging match over 'Clark's coven' case

London, Tuesday 31
Barely disguised revelations in the published diaries of Alan Clark that he seduced the two daughters of a judge while carrying on a 14-year affair with his wife are titillating the nation. The judge, James Harkess, has told his story to the *News of the World* and threatens to horsewhip Clark. The self-confessed philanderer and former defence procurement minister complains that he has been "bitterly traduced" by people he once held in affection.

May 27. Yabba dabba doo time: *The Flintstones*, starring Liz Taylor, John Goodman and Rick Moranis, is released in the US by Universal Pictures.

May 28. Glyndebourne, famous round the world for its opera, reopens with a performance of the *Marriage of Figaro* after a £30 million rebuilding.

June

1994

Su	Mo	Tu	We	Th	Fr	Sa
			1	2	3	4
5	6	7	8	9	10	11
12	13	14	15	16	17	18
19	20	21	22	23	24	25
26	27	28	29	30		

Epsom, 1
The 215th Epsom Derby is won by Erhaab, ridden by Willie Carson.

Madrid, 1
Suspected Basque separatists assassinate Brigadier General Juan Rovira.

Brisbane, 1
Wigan beat the Brisbane Broncos 20-14 to take Rugby League's World Cup back from their Australian rivals.

Cairo, 2
Colombia is chosen to lead the Nonaligned Group of nations.

Lebanon, 2
Israeli warplanes attack Hezbollah guerrillas, killing some 30 muslim fighters.

Kigali, 2
Truce talks between Rwandan army and rebel commanders fail. (→ 8)

Washington, 2
Official figures show that the US prison population reached a record 948,881 people in 1993.

Britain, 3
Animal rights militants send fire-bombs to companies connected with live animal exports, injuring three people.

Washington, 3
Exiled Haitian President Jean-Bertrand Aristide calls for military action to oust the regime in Haiti. (→ 10)

Indonesia, 3
Tidal waves caused by an earthquake kill 150 people.

Pretoria, 4
In their first rugby international since sporting relations were cut because of Pretoria's apartheid policies, England beat South Africa 32-15.

United States, 4
The former Marine officer involved in the Irangate scandal, Oliver North, wins the Virginia Republican nomination for the US Senate.

Kuwait, 4
Six men are sentenced to death for plotting to assassinate former US President George Bush.

DEATH

4. Lord Thorneycroft, British politician (*29/7/09).

Anti-terror officials die

Mull of Kintyre, Thursday 2
Twenty-five of Britain's leading counter-terrorist experts died tonight when the Chinook helicopter carrying them from Belfast to a conference at Inverness crashed in dense fog on a remote Scottish hillside. The dead included the two top MI5 officers in Ulster, one of them being John Deverell, a former deputy director-general of the Security Service. Among the senior officers of the RUC who died was Assistant Chief Constable Brian Fitzsimons. The army lost Colonel Christopher Biles, Assistant Chief of Staff, HQ Northern Ireland. The death of so many experienced officers will be a terrible blow to the fight against the IRA, and there is disbelief that they were all travelling in the same aircraft. One member of the RUC said tonight: "The force is devastated. It seems the upper echelon of the special branch is missing." First reports from the site say the Chinook hit the hillside, then cartwheeled and burnt. There were no survivors. The indications are that it was an accident and the IRA was not involved.

Author Nasrin is hunted in Bangladesh

Bangladesh, Saturday 4
With a warrant out for her arrest and Islamic fundamentalists calling for her death, Taslima Nasrin has gone underground.

Raised a Muslim, the 31-year-old author has renounced her faith and denounced Islamic society as being oppressive of women. An article in an Indian newspaper, reprinted today in *The Bangladesh Times*, quoted her as saying that the Koran should be thoroughly revised. "I'm not in favor of minor changes," she reportedly said. "It serves no purpose." This is blasphemy in the eyes of the fundamentalists and a further provocation from a woman who has written frankly about sex and criticised marriage.

Yamaha crew roars to Whitbread victory

Southampton, Friday 3
Both *Yamaha* and *New Zealand Endeavour* can claim victories in the Whitbread round-the-world yacht race. Ross Field skippered *Yamaha* across the finish line first to claim overall victory in the Whitbread 60 class with a combined time of 120 days and 14 hours. An hour later, Grant Dalton and his crew brought in *New Zealand Endeavour* to win in the Maxi class and set a course record with a time of 120 days and five hours. The last leg, from Fort Lauderdale, Florida, was a thriller. The top three boats, sailing in sight of each other for the last miles, all beat the sixth-leg record.

New US ambassador presented to Queen

London, Thursday 2
Admiral William Crowe, the new US ambassador to "the Court of St James's", presented his credentials to the Queen at Buckingham Palace today. A massive bulldog of a man, Crowe is a former chairman of the joint chiefs of staff. But, while he

looks every inch an old sailor he also speaks fluent French and German and has degrees from two universities. He is, therefore, well-equipped for his new job, but he has a hard act to follow; his predecessor, Raymond Seitz, has been the best US ambassador to London in 30 years.

June 3. US President Bill Clinton begins an eight-day European tour in Rome, where he has an audience at the Vatican with Pope John Paul II.

June
1994

Su	Mo	Tu	We	Th	Fr	Sa
			1	2	3	4
5	6	7	8	9	10	11
12	13	14	15	16	17	18
19	20	21	22	23	24	25
26	27	28	29	30		

Paris, 5
Arantxa Sanchez and Sergi Bruguera of Spain win the women's and men's finals of the French Open.

India, 5
India test fires a missile capable of reaching targets in China.

Bonn, 5
Chancellor Helmut Kohl says that he never sought an invitation to attend the D-Day ceremonies in Normandy. (→6)

China, 6
All 160 people aboard a China Northwest Airlines Tupolev Tu-154 are killed when it crashes shortly after takeoff.

Yemen, 6
Northern Yemen declares a ceasefire in its month-long civil war with the secessionist south. (→7/7)

Paris, 6
A drawing for a 1938 first edition of a Tintin comic book is auctioned for a record $100,000.

Spain, 7
Work begins on the 5.3-mile Somport tunnel under the Pyrenees that will link Spain to France.

Oxford, 8
President Clinton receives an honorary law degree at University College.

London, 8
Irish actor Pierce Brosnan is chosen to play the next James Bond.

Kigali, 8
Rwandan rebels murder the Roman Catholic Archbishop of Kigali, Vincent Nsengiyumva, and 12 other clergymen. (→23)

Washington, 10
President Clinton announces a ban on all air traffic between the US and Haiti. (→12)

Warsaw, 10
The parliament eases Poland's tough anti-abortion law, allowing women to terminate a pregnancy when they are in a difficult personal situation.

DEATHS

6. Mark McManus, British actor (*21/2/35).

6. Barry Sullivan, US actor (*1913).

Dennis Potter dies at 59

London, Tuesday 7
Dennis Potter (*17/5/35), probably the most important dramatist television has produced, died of cancer today, one week after the death of his adored wife, Margaret.

His plays were controversial; one, *Blackeyes*, was generally reviled, but he attained dramatic heights and TV popularity with others such as *The Singing Detective*, *Pennies From Heaven* and *Lipstick On Your Collar*. His writing reflected his background as a working-class university boy and a sufferer from crippling psoriasis. He knew he was dying and in a remarkable TV interview told how he was struggling to stay alive to finish two last dramas for TV.

US Congress votes for arms to Bosnia

Washington, Thursday 9
Despite opposition from the White House and the Pentagon, the House of Representatives today adopted a resolution, by a vote of 244 to 178, to force President Clinton to end support for the ban on supplying arms to the Bosnian Muslims. The resolution, which also authorises up to $200 million in arms for the Bosnians, conflicts with Senate legislation. The move is a way for the House to show its disapproval of Clinton's present policies. (→27/7)

June 10. Arise Sir Bobby: England's record scorer, with a total of 49 goals, Bobby Charlton, is knighted by Queen Elizabeth.

One more record for batsman Brian Lara

Edgbaston, Monday 6
Cricket's two most prestigious records now belong to the young West Indian batsman Brian Lara. Just 50 days ago he scored 375 against England to set a new record for a Test innings; today he completed a mammoth innings of 501 not out for Warwickshire against Durham, thus breaking Hanif Mohammed's record of 499 in a first-class innings. Lara's record came with his 72nd boundary on the penultimate ball of the game. "To achieve the highest ever total is fantastic. It's something I didn't think possible," he said later but added: "I am not yet a complete cricketer."

June 7. A long haul: 12-year-old Vicki Van Meter from Pennsylvania lands in Scotland, becoming the youngest person to fly across the Atlantic.

June 11. Thousands of Britons and numerous tourists flocked to the Mall and Horseguards Parade to watch the Queen's colourful birthday parade.

Thousands pay tribute to the heroes

Normandy, Monday 6

The flags of the 14 nations that launched the liberation of Europe from the Nazis were carried ashore from four landing craft at 6:20 this morning, 50 years to the minute after the first invasion troops landed on Normandy's shell-torn beaches. Britain's D-Day commemoration started under a weeping sky with the Queen paying tribute to the 3,935 British soldiers buried in Bayeux cemetery. The Queen and President Mitterrand laid wreaths, and Prince Philip read from *The Pilgrim's Progress*. But it was very much the day of the veterans, their families and their memories of that other day which they survived when so many around them were killed. The British commemorations ended on Arromanches beach, where more than 10,000 veterans marched past the Queen. Tens of thousands of people watched the procession from the surrounding hills where astonished German gunners had spotted the arriving invasion fleet. The Queen

The Britannia, *dwarfed by a US aircraft carrier, sets off from Portsmouth.*

President Clinton has a private moment with three American D-Day veterans.

# of Operation Overlord in Normandy

expressed the nation's thanks to the bemedalled old warriors: "It was you and your comrades and Allies fighting on other fronts who delivered Europe from that yoke of organized barbarism from which the men and women of following generations have been mercifully free." Then, as the day ended with the military bands playing "We'll Meet Again" and "Roll Out the Barrel", the old soldiers, many on sticks or in wheelchairs, slowly faded away. Further along the coast, at Beny-sur-Mer, the Canadians paid tribute to their 2,044 dead laid to rest in a cemetery among the cornfields. At Colleville cemetery, which overlooks Omaha Beach, where so many Americans died in the bloodiest fighting of D-Day, President Bill Clinton stood before the colonnade honouring the 9,386 American soldiers buried there and said: "These are the fathers we never knew, the uncles we never met, the friends who never returned, the heroes we can never repay."

A lament for the thousands of soldiers who died on the Normandy beaches.

Old soldiers stand together to pay their last respects to their fallen comrades.

June

1994

Su	Mo	Tu	We	Th	Fr	Sa
			1	2	3	4
5	6	7	8	9	10	11
12	13	14	15	16	17	18
19	20	21	22	23	24	25
26	27	28	29	30		

Switzerland, 12
Voters reject government plans to provide UN peacekeeping troops.

Port-au-Prince, 12
Haitian leader Emile Jonassaint declares a state of emergency. (→ 14/7)

Montreal, 12
Michael Schumacher wins the Canadian Grand Prix.

Moscow, 13
Yegor Gaidar, a leading advocate of economic reform, is chosen to head a new party, Democratic Choice of Russia.

London, 14
Tottenham Hotspur are banned from taking part in next year's FA Cup, will have 12 points deducted at the start of the next season and are fined £600,000 for making irregular payments to players.

Vatican, 15
The Vatican and Israel establish full diplomatic relations.

Ascot, 16
In full view of the Queen, a student is seriously injured when he is knocked down by a horse after running onto the course during the Ribblesdale Stakes. →

United States, 16
A study shows that the number of abortions performed in the US dropped to 1,529,000 in 1992, the lowest level since 1979.

France, 16
Two small-time drug dealers confess to the murder in February of the conservative MP Yann Piat.

Germany, 17
The destruction by road engineers of the historic Torgau Bridge spanning the Elbe River, where US and Soviet troops met on April 25, 1945, causes a public outcry.

DEATHS

12. Rabbi Menahem Schneerson, head of the Lubavitcher sect (*1902).

14. Henry Mancini, US composer and band leader (*16/4/24).

15. Manos Hadjidakis, Greek composer (*1926).

European elections deal yet another body blow to John Major

Voters in Britain have lifted Labour's spirits with a strong show of support.

London, Monday 13
John Major is faced with a battered and divided party today after the European Parliament election results, which saw the worst national performance by the Tories this century. They won only 18 seats of the UK's allocation of 87 while the resurgent Labour Party took 62. One MP has called for Major to go immediately while the "Europeans", led by Sir Edward Heath, and the "Euro-sceptics" square up for another battle with each side blaming the other for the disaster.

On the Continent, the Austrians voted overwhelmingly to join the EU. There were mixed signals from other countries where, in low turnouts, small radical groups gained ground, and the main parties played swings and roundabouts. (→ 16)

Striking signalmen bring chaos, rail misery to millions in Britain

London, Wednesday 15
Today's strike over pay and productivity by more than 4,000 signalmen shut down nearly all of Britain's 11,000-mile network. British Rail was able to run fewer than 500 of its normal 15,000 passenger services. Even when the 24-hour strike is over, there will be disruption as trains are wrongly positioned.

A second walk-out has been called for next Wednesday, and although many commuters simply took the day off, this rolling campaign of strikes threatens a summer of misery and frustration. (→ 22)

June 16. One sure way to turn heads at Ascot's Ladies' Day.

June 18. A farewell to arms: British, American and French troops bid a military farewell to Berlin after guarding the city for nearly a half-century.

Millions watch fall of American hero OJ Simpson

In a scene worthy of Starsky and Hutch, *the fugitive former football star is chased by police as supporters cheer.*

Los Angeles, Friday 17

A white Ford Bronco led a group of California Highway Patrol cars and a fleet of television news helicopters across the motorways of LA County as thousands of people along the roadsides stared and millions more watched on TV. In the Bronco was movie star, corporate spokesman and former football hero Orenthal James Simpson. Simpson led the pack to his home and then gave himself up. Earlier today, he failed to appear for an agreed upon arraignment on charges of murdering his former wife and another man.

Nicole Brown Simpson, 35, and Ronald Goldman, a waiter at a restaurant she frequented, were savagely murdered at Nicole Simpson's home last week.

Norman Fowler, Tory party chairman, quits

London, Thursday 16

Sir Norman Fowler stepped down from his post as Tory party chairman today to concentrate on his business affairs. He leaves without rancour. This is the second time he has departed gracefully from a major post, having resigned from the Thatcher government after 10 years for "family, domestic and personal reasons". However, his timing, on the eve of a government reshuffle, threatens further turmoil within the demoralised party. There is no obvious candidate to replace him. Backbenchers would like to see Michael Heseltine get the job, but he has made it clear he does not want it. Another struggle now looms between the right and left of the party.

World Cup fans shot dead by Protestants

Loughinisland, Saturday 18

The sounds of laughing and cheering in a bar in this predominantly Catholic village 20 miles southeast of Belfast were suddenly wiped out by the blast of gunfire and screams of the wounded and dying. As the crowd in the bar watched the television broadcast from New Jersey of Ireland's World Cup football team heading to a 1-0 victory over Italy, two men entered and began firing at random. Six people were killed and five wounded.

The Ulster Volunteer Force, an outlawed Protestant paramilitary group, claimed responsibility for the attack, the most deadly act of sectarian violence in Ulster in the last eight months. (→ 12/7)

Carter bid to defuse US-Korea nuke crisis

Washington, Saturday 18

Jimmy Carter has returned from a three-day trip to North Korea, where he met the 82-year-old Kim Il Sung. He brought a message from the country's "Great Leader" that he was ready to meet South Korean President Kim Young Sam "at any time and any place".

The summit would be the first meeting between the leaders of the two Koreas since their division in 1945. Though no advance was made toward ending the dispute over inspection of North Korea's nuclear facilities, the globe-trotting ex-president is again being hailed as a peacemaker. But the White House is put off by Carter's implication that the US would back off on seeking sanctions on North Korea without an agreement on inspections. (→ 22)

June 17. Soccer, a profound mystery to the vast majority of Americans, has come to the US with a vengeance, as President Clinton, whose daughter Chelsea is said to love the game, and 62,000 sweltering fans, many of them of European or Latin American origin, attend the opening of World Cup 1994 at Chicago's Soldier Field stadium.

June

Red faces for Moscow police as big crackdown turns into fiasco

Mobsters had been warned of the operation so few of them were rounded up.

Moscow, Wednesday 22
The Moscow police's Operation Hurricane has turned out to be all wet. About 20,000 coppers played Eliot Ness and the Untouchables in raids on casinos and hotels believed to be Russian mafia hotbeds today. But word got out, and the police tended to find closed doors – one of the suspected criminals' dens had a "Closed for Sanitary Cleaning" sign on the door. Instead of handcuffing gangsters, they ended up making arrests on minor charges. Russians view mafia crime as one of the biggest threats to their society, and the government has granted police wide powers to arrest and hold suspects.

Pop singer George Michael loses costly legal battle against Sony

London, Tuesday 21
Chart-topper George Michael sang "You gotta have faith", and he says he still believes the English legal system will deliver him from "professional slavery" to Sony. He plans to appeal today's decision that ruled his 1988 contract with the company was "reasonable and fair". Michael, who has spent £3 million on the case, argued that Sony refused to promote his album *Listen Without Prejudice* because it broke with his old image as a Top of the Pops sex symbol. His contract, which could run for another 15 years, is not in restraint of trade according to the court's ruling.

June 21. Fashion designer Kenzo marks the first day of summer by draping the Pont Neuf, in Paris, with flowers.

Crucial Corfu Euro-summit wrecked by British veto

John Major's stance has angered many of the other European Union leaders.

Corfu, Saturday 25

John Major threw the European Commission into crisis tonight when he vetoed the appointment of Jean-Luc Dehaene, the federalist Belgian prime minister, to succeed Jacques Delors as president of the commission. Major, in a defiant mood, exercised his veto despite being a minority of one in opposing Dehaene at the end of the two-day summit.

Helmut Kohl, the German chancellor, immediately called an emergency summit in Brussels on July 15 to break the deadlock. Some members insisted that Dehaene's name could be put forward again at this meeting, but the search is now on for a compromise candidate acceptable to all 12 member states.

A furious Delors accused Major of wrecking the summit, implying that he used his veto for domestic political reasons. Major denies this: "I took a decision – it wasn't easy – because I believe it was the right decision and for no other reason." But his stand has done him no harm at Westminster. "This has not been a question of John Major appeasing the Euro-sceptics," said Tory MP Sir George Gardiner, "but of stopping the Franco-German axis dictating to the rest of Europe." (→ 15/7)

Russia finally signs NATO peace accord

Brussels, Wednesday 22

Russia today became the 21st of the former Warsaw Pact states to join NATO's Partnership for Peace programme, but only after weeks of hard bargaining to ensure Russia's status as a world power. The signing of the pact by Foreign Minister Andrei Kozyrev at a ceremony in NATO headquarters was hailed by US Secretary of State Warren Christopher as "a dream which has animated this alliance and my country for more than four decades." However, hardline opposition to the pact continues in Moscow.

Nigeria crisis grows after Abiola's arrest

Lagos, Thursday 23

Moshood K O Abiola, who unofficially won the annulled Nigerian presidential election last year, was arrested at his home here today. Yesterday, the opposition leader appeared before 2,000 supporters at a rally and promised that he would form a government. Earlier this month, he declared himself president and commander-in-chief of the armed forces. After the arrest, hundreds of youths demonstrated in the city's commercial center, shouting anti-government slogans and demanding Abiola's release. (→ 18/7)

June 24. Fat yellow flyer: the Airbus A300-600 ST, the world's biggest cargo aircraft, known as the Beluga, is rolled out from its Toulouse factory.

June 23. The government decides to decommission the yacht *Britannia*, which has been in royal service since 1953 and costs £10 million a year to run.

June

1994

Su	Mo	Tu	We	Th	Fr	Sa
			1	2	3	4
5	6	7	8	9	10	11
12	13	14	15	16	17	18
19	20	21	22	23	24	25
26	27	28	29	30		

Shoreham, West Sussex, 27
A woman who came out of a hair salon with seven colours and two white stripes in her hair accepts a £4,000 out-of-court settlement in compensation for the "hairdo from hell".

Vatican, 27
Sister Emilia Ehrlich is the first woman to be named by the pope to a senior post in a synod of bishops; she will assist in running the October synod, on the life of priests and nuns.

London, 27
After frosts in southern Brazil, coffee prices reach their highest level in seven years on commodity markets here and in New York.

London, 27
Michael Nazir Ali, who holds British and Pakistani passports, is chosen to be the next Bishop of Rochester; he will be the first non-white diocesan bishop of the Church of England.

Mexico City, 28
Celebrations for Mexico's advance in the World Cup after drawing with Italy 1-1 are marred by outbreaks of drunken violence; two people are killed and scores wounded.

Pontiac, Michigan, 28
The turf installed at the Silverdome must be removed after the last World Cup game here today; the Michigan host committee is looking for takers.

Tokyo, 29
Tomiichi Murayama becomes Japan's first Socialist prime minister since 1948.

London, 30
Prince Charles unveils a plaque commemorating the centenary of Tower Bridge.

Hong Kong, 30
China and Britain conclude arrangements for the handover of defence sites when China resumes sovereignty of Hong Kong. →

United States, 30
The population of US prisons exceeds 1 million for the first time; there are 373 prisoners for every 100,000 US residents.

Paris, 30
The International Earth Rotation Service advances the world's atomic clocks by one second.

Pro-democracy demonstrators march in Algiers despite attack

Algiers, Wednesday 29
In the battle for Algeria, mostly fought between the government and Islamic militants, there are those who oppose both sides. At about noon today, 15,000 demonstrators prepared to protest against both groups and to demand democracy. As the march was starting, two explosions and then gunfire scattered the crowd; 64 people were wounded, two very seriously. When a semblance of calm was regained, the marchers, some bloodied, went on. The demonstration was scheduled on the second anniversary of the assassination of President Mohamed Boudiaf to refocus attention on the killing and to demand an investigation to find whether a conspiracy was behind it.

A least one gunman opened fire on the peaceful marchers, injuring 64 people.

CIA's 'Caspian Monster' may be the hybrid aircraft of the future

United States, June
A mysterious craft sighted by US spy satellites plying the Caspian Sea was nicknamed the Caspian Monster by the CIA in the 1970s. The Russians, who designed and built it, called it the Ekranoplan. Half-boat, half-airplane, it used a cushion of air to zoom across land and sea. Perestroika in the USSR nearly doomed the project. Now, American defence contractors are interested in working with the Russians to develop a Super Ekranoplan able to carry 1,500 tons of cargo or 2,000 passengers. The cost of the project would be $15 billion, with each Ekranoplan costing $400 million to build.

Bonn ban on British beef angers London

London, Tuesday 28
A furious row erupted today when Germany announced a six-month ban on British beef, claiming it could be contaminated with "mad cow disease". Gillian Shephard, the Agriculture minister, pointed out that the European Commission had ruled there were already adequate safeguards at British slaughterhouses and said the government would demand redress in the European Court. She also voiced suspicions that the ban was revenge for John Major's Corfu veto. (→ 18/7)

June 28. Nigel Mansell at the controls of a Formula One car for the first time since 1992. The winner of 30 Grand Prix is to return to F1 racing.

Prince of Wales says divorce will not block accession to throne

London, Thursday 30
In a remarkably frank ITV documentary marking the 25th anniversary of his investiture, the Prince of Wales said last night he had no plans to divorce but insisted that he would not regard divorce as an impediment to becoming king. In an uneasy passage, he confirmed that he had been unfaithful but only after his marriage "became irretrievably broken down". Of Camilla Parker-Bowles, he said only that she was "a great friend". Not surprisingly, the prince was more at ease when the presenter, Jonathan Dimbleby, turned to his less publicised interests. Inevitably, however, reaction is centering on his revelations about his marriage. If he had hoped to quell public curiosity, he has failed.

Prince Charles and Camilla Parker-Bowles sharing a quiet moment at sea.

Whitewater rulings favour Bill Clinton

Washington, Thursday 30
No White House officials will be charged with breaking laws in connection with their receiving briefings on an investigation into Whitewater said Robert Fiske, the special counsel, in the first findings of his investigation into the affair.

The Whitewater affair takes its name from an Arkansas real estate development in which President Clinton invested while governor of the state. James McDougal, who was a partner in Whitewater with Clinton, ran Madison Guaranty Savings and Loan, which later went bankrupt. It is the investigation into that failure which the administration was accused of influencing.

World Cup drama as Diego Maradona is banned for drug violation

The 33-year-old Argentine star is accused of having taken drugs to lose weight.

Foxboro, Mass, Thursday 30
The biggest name in football has been suspended from the game for using a banned drug. Diego Maradona, the Argentinian team captain, apparently took a cocktail of five different types of ephedrine, a drug commonly used as a decongestant to treat colds, allergies and asthma. He may have taken the drug in order to lose weight for the World Cup, but it is also used as a stimulant, working like the naturally produced adrenalin in the body, increasing blood pressure and heartbeat. The Argentine FA president said that Maradona had used a nasal spray before the game because he felt ill.

USSR's A-bombers carried fake bombs

Moscow, Thursday 30
Major General Anatoli Solovyov, deputy commander of the Russian Air Force's long range nuclear bomber units, revealed today that throughout the Cold War these units, targeted on Western cities, had never flown with real nuclear bombs. In an article in *Literaturnaya Gazeta*, he says that because of fear of accidents Soviet ground crews practiced loading nuclear weapons but always replaced them with dummies before the bombers took off, even during the periods of greatest tension.

Patten reform plan approved in Hong Kong

Hong Kong, Thursday 30
Governor Chris Patten's constitutional reform Bill was approved by the Legislative Council by 32 votes to 24 after 15 hours of impassioned debate and manoeuvre in which the Bill came close to defeat. Finally passed in the early hours, the new law, which gives limited democracy to the colony, is a triumph for Patten and a loss of face for Beijing. Foreign Secretary Douglas Hurd said the people of Hong Kong had got what they wanted, "open and fair electoral arrangements". China, however, has vowed to expunge them when it takes over in 1997.

June 30. The sun is out for the second day of the Henley Royal Regatta, attended by many Australians who came to encourage a team from home.

July

1994

Su	Mo	Tu	We	Th	Fr	Sa
					1	2
3	4	5	6	7	8	9
10	11	12	13	14	15	16
17	18	19	20	21	22	23
24	25	26	27	28	29	30
31						

Geneva, 1
The World Health Organization says the number of AIDS cases worldwide has increased from 2.5 to 4 million over the past year.

London, 2
Ahmed Zahrani, former vice consul at the Saudi consulate in Houston, Texas, applies for political asylum, claiming Riyadh threatened him after he wrote a book on Saudi politics.

Jericho, 3
A Palestinian militant group opposed to peace with Israel overrides the PLO radio station Voice of Palestine, broadcasting anti-Arafat taunts; he is called a "clown" and a "traitor". (→ 25)

Paris, 3
The leader of the French Socialists says the party is in such bad financial straits that they must sell their Paris headquarters and move somewhere cheaper.

Kigali, 4
The rebel Rwandan Patriotic Front captures the Rwandan capital. (→ 22)

Lausanne, 6
American Leroy Burrell breaks the 100-metre sprint record with a time of 9.85 seconds.

Japan, 7
The sumo wrestling association bans the practice of using silicone scalp implants to reach the minimum height of 68 inches.

Dublin, 7
The returning Irish World Cup team are welcomed home by thousands of cheering fans.

London, 9
Warwickshire beat Worcestershire by six wickets to win the Benson & Hedges Cup Final.

Gleneagles, 9
Golfer Carl Mason wins the Scottish Open.

DEATHS

2. Marion Williams, American gospel singer (*1927).

3. Lew Hoad, Australian tennis player (*23/11/34).

6. Cameron Mitchell, American actor (*4/11/1894).

Yasser Arafat ends exile

Thousands cheer the PLO chief as he returns after an absence of 27 years.

Gaza, Friday 1
Yasser Arafat crossed the Egyptian border with the Gaza Strip today, ending 27 years of exile from the territories now coming under Palestinian self-rule. With tears in his eyes, he kissed the ground then waved to the crowd of ecstatic supporters. His motorcade hurried on to the city of Gaza, where he addressed a crowd of 100,000 Palestinians. He promised to help build a new homeland and said more courage was needed from Jews and Palestinians to keep the peace. He listed holy places in Israeli-held territory where Palestinians would go to pray, finishing with Jerusalem. His words were met with cheers but were certainly worrisome for Israel, which insists that the city shall remain their undivided capital. (→ 3)

A World Cup player is killed in Colombia

Medellin, Colombia, Saturday 2
Colombian soccer star Andres Escobar was shot dead in the parking lot of a nightclub here at 3:30 this morning. He had returned to Colombia after his team failed to make it to the second round in the World Cup, having lost 3-1 to Romania, then 2-1 to the US. In the game against the Americans, the ball bounced off his leg to score a goal against his own team. Witnesses reported hearing one of the murderers say, "Thanks for the own-goal," before firing on him and shout "Goal! Goal!" as the shots rang out. Police are looking into the possibility that two suspects arrested this afternoon had lost money betting on the team, which was a favourite to win the championship.

Tory riposte against new Franglais follies

London, Tuesday 5
Tory MP Anthony Steen, reacting to the French government's latest attempt to ban Franglais, introduced a French Words (Prohibition) Bill today. He told the House of Commons: "Forget words like baguette or croissant. No nouvelle cuisine. All viveurs will be banned." The House, displaying admirable sangfroid, voted non.

Sampras and Conchita Martinez of Spain win Wimbledon finals

Congratulations for Conchita, 22.

Wimbledon, Sunday 3
On a scorching afternoon when the temperature on the Centre Court was measured at 116 degrees, the 22-year-old American, Pete Sampras, retained his singles championship by overpowering the temperamental Croat Goran Ivanisevic, 7-6, 7-6, 6-0. There were hardly any rallies; the match, settled by booming serves, was judged boring by those who like to see some finesse in their tennis. Yesterday, Martina Navratilova attempted to crown her brilliant career by taking her tally of Wimbledon singles trophies to 10 before retiring from the game. It was not to be. At 37, she was beaten by the 22-year-old Spaniard Conchita Martinez, 6-4, 3-6, 6-3. Martina was cheered off the court.

Pete's second Wimbledon victory.

Dictator Kim Il Sung dies

July 1. Twenty-five years ago, the Queen placed a gold coronet on Charles's head during his investiture as Prince of Wales at Caernarvon Castle.

Pyongyang, Friday 8
President Kim Il Sung of North Korea, the 20th century's longest-ruling dictator, died today apparently of a heart attack, on the eve of crucial nuclear talks with the US. He was 82. He was the only leader North Korea has ever known, and he shut the country off from the rest of the world. It was he who precipitated the Korean war by invading the South, and when that ended in stalemate, he retreated behind a tissue of lies, pronouncing the greatness of communism's victory in his fiefdom. For years the only glimpse the West obtained of him was from the full-page advertisements he took at vast expense in Western newspapers to extoll his virtues as the "Great Leader". Recently, facing economic collapse, he had become a danger again, threatening to develop nuclear weapons and attempting to blackmail the US. His son, Kim Jong Il, has been groomed as his successor. The world waits to see what path he will follow. (→ 13)

July 2. Chris Boardman of England wins the prologue of the Tour de France at Lille, finishing a full 15 seconds ahead of Miguel Indurain of Spain.

Yemeni troops seize the port city of Aden

Aden, Thursday 7
The government of northern Yemen has proclaimed victory in the two-month civil war with the secessionist south. Most fighting had ended by this morning, and the leaders of the south have fled the country. By this afternoon, residents of this southern port city were on the streets waving victory signs at the northern troops. But the secessionist leaders vow to continue their fight. It is feared that a guerrilla war could continue and even spread havoc and violence to neighbouring oil-producing states such as Saudi Arabia.

Li, China's premier, heckled in Germany

Munich, Friday 8
Behind closed doors, where Li Peng has wrapped up about £2.3 billion worth of trade agreements with German firms, the Chinese prime minister's visit has been a success. In public, it has been a nightmare. For the third day in a row, he has backed out of an official visit because of protests against his country's abysmal human rights record. Today, he cancelled a boat ride on the Tegernsee. He thus will not have to look upon the two six-foot Liberty statues protestors planned to mount on the docks in memory of Tiananmen.

July 4. Heading your way: Eire midfielder Roy Keane fights it out with Dutchman Rob Witschge during Ireland's 2-0 defeat at Orlando, Florida.

July
1994

Su	Mo	Tu	We	Th	Fr	Sa
					1	2
3	4	5	6	7	8	9
10	11	12	13	14	15	16
17	18	19	20	21	22	23
24	25	26	27	28	29	30
31						

CIS, 10
In presidential elections of two former Soviet republics, incumbents are ousted and candidates who favour closer ties with Russia are elected: Leonid Kuchma is the new president of Ukraine, and Alexander Lukashenko is elected in Belarus.

Cambodia, 11
After being outlawed by the Cambodian parliament, the Khmer Rouge proclaims a "provisional government".

Haiti, 11
Human rights monitors from the UN and Organization of American States are ordered to leave the country. (→ 14)

Lancashire, 12
A lorry containing two tons of explosives in false compartments is seized at Heysham ferryport; police believe the IRA planned to detonate it in London. (→ 24)

Ukraine, 12
An offer by the G7 of $200 million to shut down the Chernobyl nuclear plant is refused.

Hong Kong, 12
The government says 42,000 people applied for 13,000 British passports under a special scheme before the colony reverts to Chinese rule in 1997.

North Korea, 13
Kim Il Jong takes all three top government positions previously occupied by his late father. (→ 13/8)

London, 14
The Queen opens the new, £150 million headquarters of MI6, "Babylon on the Thames".

Nigeria, 14
Strikes to protest against the military government bring the country to a halt. (→ 18)

London, 14
The Crown Prosecution Service says it will not prosecute soldiers on charges of war crimes during the 1982 Falklands conflict due to insufficient evidence.

Blackburn, 15
Striker Chris Sutton signs a record-breaking £5 million, five-year contract with Blackburn Rovers.

Junta remains defiant as US Navy warships steam towards Haiti

Port-au-Prince, Thursday 14
The US Coast Guard has picked up 15,107 Haitians fleeing the country in their makeshift boats this month, bringing the year's total to 23,469.

Opinion remains divided in Washington over whether an invasion should be carried out. Nevertheless, yesterday the Marines carried out a mock invasion and evacuation exercise on the Bahamian island of Great Inagua to simulate the kind of operation they would perform in Haiti when and if President Clinton gives the go-ahead. Despite the increasing pressure, Lt-Gen Cédras says he will not step down until the judge he installed as president is recognised by the international community. (→ 31)

President Bill Clinton tells 100,000 Germans: 'Berlin ist frei'

Berlin, Tuesday 12
President Clinton stood with Chancellor Kohl before the Brandenburg Gate today and, emulating John F Kennedy's statement, "Ich bin ein Berliner", told the huge crowd, "Berlin ist frei". He reassured them: "America is on your side – now and forever." This was the last day of his week-long European tour, the day on which he decommissioned the US garrison in Berlin. With the Berlin Wall torn down, his aides struggled to find an evocative backdrop for his speech. Despite their efforts, it was apparent to the Berliners that he is no Kennedy.

The US leader speaks to Berliners at the city's historic Brandenburg Gate.

July 10. Damon Hill wins the 61-lap Grand Prix at Silverstone after Schumacher is given a five-second penalty for overtaking during a warm-up lap.

Cash for questions affair sparks storm

Westminster, Tuesday 12
Parliament is in uproar over the accusations that two Tory MPs, Graham Riddick and David Tredinnick, accepted money to ask "commercial" questions in the House. They have been suspended from their posts, and the Speaker, Betty Boothroyd, is considering what form an inquiry should take. The storm raged on today after the release of tape recordings of alleged conversations between the MPs and a journalist posing as a businessman. The MPs are apparently heard agreeing that cheques for £1,000 should be sent to their homes.

Franco-American AIDS row finally settled

Vindication for Professor Luc Montagnier of the Pasteur Institute in Paris.

Paris, Tuesday 12
The American National Institutes of Health yesterday admitted that a virus isolated by Luc Montagnier's team of scientists at the Pasteur Institute was used to develop an HIV test kit. The French will now receive more royalties on sales of the kits. The acknowledgement ends a decade of quarrels over who found the virus first. Montagnier said today that he was happy with the recognition, but "for me, one of the essential points is that this accord ends an affair that was poisoning scientific relations." He added: "The important thing now is to find a medical solution for the Third World and increase international action against this pandemic."

Defence review calls for big UK force cuts

London, Thursday 14
Drastic new reductions in the armed forces were announced today, but this time the axe is falling on the "tail" rather than front-line forces. Nearly 19,000 jobs and dozens of bases will be cut in the support services, ranging from the Ministry of Defence to spares depots. Defence Secretary Malcolm Rifkind sweetened the pill by announcing a £5 billion programme of weapons orders, which could include fitting non-nuclear submarines with Tomahawk cruise missiles.

Luxembourg's premier to be EU president

A pair of Jacks: Jacques Delors congratulates his successor, Jacques Santer.

Brussels, Friday 15
European Union leaders today unanimously appointed Jacques Santer, Prime Minister of Luxembourg, to succeed Jacques Delors as president of the EU. The decision ends three weeks of sour debate following John Major's veto of Jean-Luc Dehaene, the Belgian prime minister. Cynics point out that Santer is just as much a federalist as Dehaene, but Major argued tonight that Santer is "a reconciler" who shares Britain's views on subsidiarity, the principle of minimum interference by Brussels, and wants to see the Community enlarged. "I have always regarded him as a healing force, not a dividing force." This view of Santer is not widely shared.

Baby Abbie is found after 16-day search

Nottingham, Saturday 16
Abbie Humphries, snatched 16 days ago when she was only four hours old, has been recovered and reunited with her parents, Roger and Karen Humphries. A tip-off led police searchers to a house only a mile from the Queen's Medical Centre, where a bogus nurse carried off Abbie while her mother rested. A 22-year-old woman will appear in court tomorrow charged with abduction. Abbie has been well-cared for. At a press conference, she yawned in the arms of her overjoyed parents.

July 14. During the annual Bastille Day celebrations, German troops march on the Champs Elysées for the first time since the end of World War II.

July 14. Lady Sarah Armstrong-Jones, 30, wearing a Jasper Conran dress, marries Daniel Chatto, 37, at St Stephen Walbrook Church in the City.

July

1994

Su	Mo	Tu	We	Th	Fr	Sa
					1	2
3	4	5	6	7	8	9
10	11	12	13	14	15	16
17	18	19	20	21	22	23
24	25	26	27	28	29	30
31						

Turnberry, 17
Zimbabwean golfer Nick Price wins the British Open.

Burma, 17
U Khun Sa, the notorious "Golden Triangle" opium warlord, offers to give himself up in return for independence of Shan State from Burma.

Los Angeles, 18
Taxi driver Juan Blanco gets a $1,000 dollar reward and a meeting with Brazilian goalkeeper Claudio Taffarel after returning the World Cup gold medal and $60,000 in cash that Taffarel had left in his taxi.

London, 18
A poll shows British firms are Europe's latest payers, taking 23 days to pay bills as opposed to the average of 14 days.

Bonn, 18
Germany abandons its ban on British beef.

London, 18
Richard Ingrams, founder and editor of The Oldie, announces that the loss-making magazine is being retired.

Rome, 18
A 62-year-old becomes the oldest woman to give birth; a donor's egg, fertilised by her husband's sperm, had been implanted in her uterus.

London, 19
Spy Kim Philby's possessions are auctioned at Sotheby's; 11 letters from novelist Graham Greene fetch £23,000.

London, 20
The Dean of Westminster says Oscar Wilde will be honoured with a plaque in Westminster Abbey's Poets' Corner.

London, 22
The Marquess of Blandford, who has been repeatedly jailed on drug charges, is stripped of the right to manage Blenheim Palace and his family's 11,500-acre estate when his father dies.

DEATHS

17. Jean Borotra, "The Bounding Basque", tennis champion (*13/8/1898).

19. James Joll, British historian (*1918).

19. Han Xu, Chinese diplomat (*1924).

Brazilians win their fourth World Cup

Heading for the top: Brazil easily dominated Sweden at the Pasadena Rose Bowl, winning the July 13 semifinal 1-0.

Pasadena, Sunday 17
After two hours of unadventurous play on both sides which emphasized defence over fancy footwork, Brazil and Italy were still at a 0-0 draw. For the first time, the World Cup final would have to be decided by penalty shootout. Italy's sweeper Franco Baresi, playing for the first time since his arthroscopic knee surgery after the second game of the cup, sent the first try way over the bar. The two teams traded hits and misses, and on Italy's last kick the Brazilians were up 3-2. Italian forward Roberto Baggio, visibly suffering from a hamstring injury, repeated Baresi's high-flying miss. Thus the Brazilians, without scoring a real goal, became the first team to have won four World Cup titles.

Italy's hero: Forward Roberto Baggio scored both goals in his team's 2-1 semifinal win over Bulgaria on July 13.

in penalty shootout after 120 scoreless minutes

Brazil midfielder Dunga brandishes the cherished trophy as he leads his teammates for a final victory lap after their historic, but sadly goalless, win at Pasadena.

Despite criticism of the conservatism of Brazilian trainer Carlos Alberto Parriera's game – even the legendary Pelé weighed in against his style – Brazilians are now singing his praises. Fifteen thousand celebrated in this California city's Colorado Boulevard, and the party back home will not let up until well after the team have returned. As Parriera himself put it: "I'm like Frank Sinatra: I did it my way."

World Cup USA is being hailed as a smashing success. Two billion people watched the final on television around the world. In a country where footballers score touchdowns and wear more protective gear than riot squads, attendance at the 52 matches set World Cup records. More than 94,000 people came to the Rose Bowl for the final. Total attendance was 3,567,415 – more than 68,000 per game – compared to the 2.5 million who turned out for Italia 90. The millions were cheerful and well behaved as well; the feared hooliganism never materialised.

For a month stadiums in Boston, New York, Detroit, Chicago, Dallas, Orlando, Los Angeles and Pasadena have been rocked by the cheers of multi-hued fans.

Argentina bomb attack against Jews

At least 96 people died in the devastating terrorist attack in Buenos Aires.

Buenos Aires, Monday 18
A powerful car bomb levelled a seven-floor building that housed two of Argentina's principal Jewish organizations. At least 96 people were killed and hundreds injured and made homeless by the explosion that devastated several large apartment blocks. The attack comes 28 months after a car bomb at the Israeli embassy here killed 30 people.

A radical Islamic group based in Lebanon, the Partisans of God, claimed responsibility for the attack. As the investigation into the bombing gets underway, Argentina is closing its borders. Israel is sending agents from Mossad, their secret service, police bomb experts and army specialists to help the Argentinian police in the investigation. (→ 26)

Pro-Abiola violence spreading in Nigeria

Lagos, Monday 18
Nigeria's political crisis deepened today with 20 people reported dead in sporadic outbreaks of violence as the country entered its third week of a strike by oil workers. The strikers are demanding an end to military rule and the release of Chief Moshood Abiola, who won last year's annulled presidential election.

Many banks, offices and shops are closed as workers stay at home, either in support of the strike or because there is no public transport. Teachers are refusing to work and many schools are closed. Chief Abiola was denied bail this week by a court trying him for treason after he proclaimed himself president in defiance of the generals. (→ 5/8)

South African cricket team back at Lords

London, Thursday 21
There were emotional scenes at Lord's today when the South Africans returned to the home of cricket for their first Test match in England in 24 years. Kepler Wessels celebrated in style, scoring a century, and coach Mike Procter waved his country's new flag from the pavilion. It was strictly against the rules, but today, nobody cared. (→ 24)

July 17. Naomi Campbell models a slinky pink evening gown at Gianni Versace's Paris show.

Ban on foetal ovaries as an infertility cure

London, Wednesday 20
The use of eggs and ovarian tissue from aborted foetuses for the treatment of infertility was banned today by the Human Fertilisation and Embryology Authority, which licenses all test tube baby clinics. Professor Sir Colin Campbell, chairman of the authority, said: "We think it would be dangerous to use foetal tissue because it could threaten the life of the woman receiving the transfer, and we do not know the effect on the child who would be born as a result."

Painter Delvaux dies

Furnes, Belgium, Wednesday 20
Belgian painter Paul Delvaux, born on September 23, 1897, died today. One of the last of the great Surrealists, he was influenced by his fellow countryman René Magritte and by Giorgio di Chirico. His early and most well known paintings featured nude women, sometimes with fully-clothed men looking at them, and are often set in deserted railway stations. His fascination with railway stations began in his childhood, and he was given a fitting tribute in 1984 when he was made honourary chief of the station in the university town of Louvain.

South Africa is back in the Commonwealth

A happy day for Archbishop Tutu.

London, Wednesday 20
The Queen Mother joined heads of state and politicians from all round the world in Westminster Abbey today to celebrate South Africa's return to the Commonwealth after 33 years in the wilderness. There was a mood of joy in the abbey which, at one stage, was filled with the sound of South African township jazz.

Archbishop Desmond Tutu compared the return with the tale of the prodigal son. He said South Africa had squandered her riches during the years of apartheid, but international pressure and the struggles of her people had finally brought the country back to its senses. "Like a prodigal, she has returned home and is getting a right royal welcome and can only say 'Wow'."

Mitterrand's health in doubt after operation

Paris, Tuesday 19
François Mitterrand received visitors this morning and discussed poetry and state affairs after having undergone his second prostate operation in two years. The president's doctor said the operation was to remove scar tissue in his urinary tract – a side effect of his 1992 operation for prostate cancer – that was causing him discomfort.

The Elysée is trying to squelch rumours that the 77-year-old president may be in much poorer health than official government reports indicate. A leading article on the front page of the daily paper *Le Monde* this evening blamed the rumours on the Elysée's failure to keep the public informed on the progression of his treatment and his health. Mitterrand had promised "transparency" on the issue, and the paper criticised the information released by the president's doctors as "soothing" rather than frank and substantial.

Major reshuffles his beleaguered Cabinet

London, Wednesday 20

John Major, seeking to introduce some life into his inert administration, acted in unusually ruthless fashion today. Twelve ministers and four whips were sacked or resigned, and in a move which surprised everybody, he appointed the little known Jeremy Hanley as the Tory party chairman. Hanley, son of actors Jimmy Hanley and Dinah Sheridan, is joined by Michael Dobbs, author of *House of Cards*, as deputy chairman. There was no place for the other novelist, Lord Archer. Only two women were promoted; Angela Browning becomes a junior agriculture minister and Baroness Miller a junior whip. The anti-Maastricht rebels got nothing.

Tony Blair wins race to lead Labour

London, Thursday 21

Tony Blair has been elected leader of the Labour Party in a landslide, winning more than half the votes in all three sections of the party: the MPs, the constituencies and the trade unions. He easily beat John Prescott, who, in a separate vote, was elected deputy leader. Blair, at 41, is the party's youngest ever leader. He is a modernist, far removed from the dinosaurs of old-fashioned socialism, and he regards his victory as a mandate to continue the reforms started by his predecessors, Neil Kinnock and the late John Smith. In a passionate speech tonight, he told a triumphant meeting he would not rest until he had put Labour "in its rightful place – in government again."

Spectacular space drama as comet batters Jupiter

Friday 22

Collisions of astral bodies are a banal event given the age of the universe. But in human terms, the battering that the planet Jupiter took this week as comet Shoemaker-Levy 9 crashed into it was a unique event. For the first time, humans were able to watch the collision of two solar system bodies.

The comet came into the orbit of the solar system's largest planet two years ago and was broken up into thousands of pieces, 21 of which were large enough to count. The first of these hit the planet last Saturday, and though it was one of the smaller fragments, it left a black streak half the size of the Earth and produced a fireball some 1,200 miles wide. Fragment G, estimated to be 2.5 miles across, hit Monday with the explosive force of 6 million megatons of TNT – the Earth's entire nuclear arsenal is around 80,000 megatons. Telescopes were blinded by the superheated gas bubble – 50 times as luminous as the planet – produced by the impact of Fragment H. The last of the big pieces hit Jupiter today, creating a scar twice the size of our planet.

Scientists are now analysing the event to find clues to the composition of the Jovian atmosphere and to how similar collisions may have influenced Earth's development.

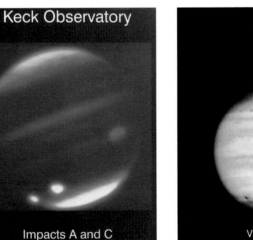

Keck Observatory

Impacts A and C

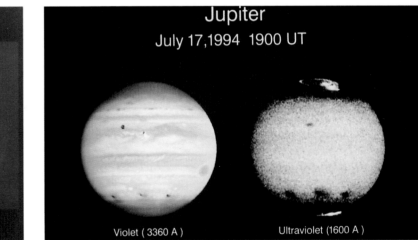

Jupiter
July 17,1994 1900 UT

Violet (3360 A)   Ultraviolet (1600 A)

After killings, cholera now decimates Rwanda's gaunt refugees

Zaire, Friday 22

Some 2.5 million refugees have fled violence-ravaged Rwanda, most just over the western border to Zaire. The teeming camps in Goma, where more than a million people are living in horrible conditions, are now suffering from an outbreak of cholera. Today, UN Secretary-General Butros Butros Ghali said the tragedy was reaching "unimaginable proportions" and called for $434 million in international aid. US President Clinton promised $185 million and sent military transport planes with medical supplies. (→ 21/8)

1994

Su	Mo	Tu	We	Th	Fr	Sa
					1	2
3	4	5	6	7	8	9
10	11	12	13	14	15	16
17	18	19	20	21	22	23
24	25	26	27	28	29	30
31						

Donegal, 24
Sinn Fein replies to the Downing Street Declaration, saying the Anglo-Irish peace plan for Ulster has "negative and contradictory elements". (→11/8)

Dakar, 24
Senegal grants asylum to Sir Dawda Jawara, the president of Gambia, who was ousted by a military coup two days ago.

Paris, 24
Spanish cyclist Miguel Indurain wins the Tour de France for the fourth straight year.

London, 24
The South African cricket team beat England by 365 runs in their first victory at Lord's in 59 years. (→30)

Cambodia, 26
The Khmer Rouge attack a train and take more than 200 passengers captive; most are released, but three Westerners are held hostage. (→7/8)

London, 27
The government says it may take legal action against the European Commission's decision to approve a 20 billion franc (£2.4 billion) bailout of Air France by the French government.

London, 28
The Lord's Select Committee on European Communities says that EU taxpayers are being cheated by "massive and growing" fraud.

Frankfurt, 28
Three 19th-century masterpieces, two by Turner on loan from the Tate, are stolen from the Schirn Gallery; the paintings are valued at £28 million.

London, 29
German World Cup team striker Jurgen Klinsmann signs a £2 million, two-year contract with Tottenham Hotspur.

DEATHS

29. Dorothy Hodgkin, British chemist (*29/7/1894).

30. Robin Cook, British novelist (*12/6/31).

31. Caitlin Thomas, wife of Welsh poet Dylan Thomas (*8/12/13).

Jordan and Israel end state of war

Washington, Monday 25
Under a burning summer sun, King Hussein of Jordan and Prime Minister Yitzhak Rabin of Israel signed a declaration to end the 46-year state of war between the Arab kingdom and the Jewish state.

Today's ceremony on the South Lawn of the White House was witnessed by President Clinton, who promised the continued help of the United States in extending peace in the Middle East. King Hussein said: "Out of all the days of my life, I do not believe there is one such as this." Rabin remembered the "fallen in the wars on both sides" and stated his prayer that lives of Israeli and Jordanian children "will be different than ours". (→8/8)

Jordan's King Hussein and Israeli premier Yitzhak Rabin (right) seal the pact.

Islamic groups bring terror to London as Israeli embassy is attacked

The car bomb exploded near the embassy in Kensington, injuring 14 people.

London, Tuesday 26
Middle Eastern terrorism returned to the streets of London today when a woman "of Mediterranean appearance" carrying a Harrod's bag penetrated the security round the Israeli embassy and set off a car bomb, injuring 14 people, damaging the embassy and breaking windows in nearby Kensington Palace.

It is feared that this is the start of a campaign against Israeli targets in London designed to undermine the Middle East peace process. The Israelis blame pro-Iranian extremists of the Hezbollah movement.

July 26. Terry Scott (*4/5/27), the much-loved comedian who won fame as the disaster-prone co-star of *Terry and June*, dies.

Mystery of O solved

New York, Monday 25
The mystery of *The Story of O* has been solved after 40 years. The author of the erotic novel from which a controversial film was made in 1975 is revealed in the current issue of *The New Yorker*. When published in 1954, the name on the title page was Pauline Réage, but critics refused to believe that the sado-masochistic fantasies in the story could have been written by a woman. But they were. Dominique Aury, a French writer who was the lover of Jean Paulhan, an *Académie française* member, says she wrote the book to keep Paulhan's interest. It must have worked; the couple stayed together until his death at the age of 83.

July 28. Lord Delfont, impresario and show-business legend, dies. He was born Boris Winogradsky (*5/9/09) in the Crimea.

UN approves US-led invasion of Haiti

New York, Sunday 31
The United Nations Security Council has authorised a US-led invasion of Haiti to drive out the military government and restore the country's exiled president, Jean-Bertrand Aristide, to power.

This "final call", in the words of the US envoy to the UN, Madeleine Albright, for the junta to step down includes no deadline; the timing of the invasion would be left up to President Clinton. Albright said the resolution was a message from the international community to Raoul Cédras and his officers: "You can depart voluntarily and soon, or you can depart involuntarily and soon. The sun is setting on your ruthless ambition." (→6/8)

Furious anti-Aristide, anti-American demonstrators march in Port-au-Prince.

Atherton to stay on as England's captain

London, Saturday 30
Michael Atherton will stay on as England's cricket captain despite the furore caused by his action in the Test against South Africa when the television cameras caught him drying his hand with dirt in his pocket before polishing the ball. He revealed yesterday that, while hiding away after being fined £2,000 for not revealing to the match referee that he had dirt in his pocket, he had considered resigning. But, he said, "It would have been for the wrong reasons – to give heed to the media clamour. I didn't think that was the correct way to go about things. In my own mind my intentions and actions were trustworthy."

Bosnia tension rises as Serbs get tough

Sarajevo, Wednesday 27
In another move to tighten the noose round this embattled city, the Serbs have told the UN that the only civilian and commercial traffic route into the city must be closed. After turning down the latest peace plan, the Serbs have become increasingly recalcitrant, firing at flights into Sarajevo and flouting the ban on the use of heavy weapons at Gorazde. The Contact Group countries must now decide whether to punish the Serbs. (→27/8)

Kinnock to be new European Commissioner

London, Friday 29
Neil Kinnock, the former Labour leader, has landed a plum job as one of Britain's two commissioners to the European Union. It is a remarkable comeback for Kinnock, 52, whose political career seemed to be at an end when, overconfident, he was defeated by John Major in the 1992 general election. He will now earn a basic salary of £140,000, almost twice as much as the prime minister. His wife, Glenys, is already in Brussels as a MEP for Southeast Wales. Kinnock says he aims to make a "constructive contribution".

Panic in Moscow as company collapses

Moscow, Friday 29
Some 10,000 angry investors in the Russian company MMM stormed the commodities exchange today to try to sell their worthless shares. When prices were rising, the shares had attracted from 5 to 10 million shareholders, but the company was little more than a pyramid scheme, in which value grew only as people bought into it. Yesterday MMM promised to buy back the shares at 125,000 rubles (about £40), but today the price was cut to 950 (30p).

July 31. Anne Shelton, famous as the 'Forces Favorite', dies. Born on Nov. 10, 1923, she sang the English version of *Lili Marlene*.

July 31. Dutch driver Jos Verstappen is unhurt as flames engulf his Benetton-Ford during the German Grand Prix.

August
1994

Su	Mo	Tu	We	Th	Fr	Sa
	1	2	3	4	5	6
7	8	9	10	11	12	13
14	15	16	17	18	19	20
21	22	23	24	25	26	27
28	29	30	31			

Norwich, 1
A fire in Norwich Central Library destroys irreplaceable historic documents and more than 100,000 books.

Ootlewah, Tennessee, 1
The amateur women's golf team of Britain and Ireland draw 9-9 with the Americans to keep the Curtis Cup.

Warsaw, 1
At commemorations of the Warsaw uprising against the Nazis, German President Roman Herzog apologises for the suffering Germany inflicted on Poland in World War II.

Washington, 2
The Congressional Research Service says that the US is the biggest supplier of arms to the Third World; Britain is second and Russia third.

London, 2
Dick Best is sacked as coach of England's rugby team; manager Jack Rowell succeeds him.

Paris, 2
France gives the green light to restart the nuclear reactor Superphenix, which has been closed four years for repairs.

Vatican, 2
The Vatican newspaper blames Italians' "selfishness" for the fact that the country has the lowest birthrate in Europe: 1.21 children per woman.

Iran, 4
After parliament defeated a Bill to make the town of Qazvin a provincial capital, riots break out in the city and at least four people are killed.

Lagos, 5
Jailed opposition leader Moshood Abiola refuses a government offer of release from prison because the conditions for his freedom include renouncing politics.

Westminster, 5
Labour MP Barbara Roche says that 260 military personnel have been dismissed since 1990 for being homosexual.

DEATHS

4. Giovanni Spadolini, former Italian premier (*21/6/25).

6. Domenico Modugno, Italian singer and composer who wrote "Volare" (*9/1/28).

A marriage made in Hollywood: Lisa Marie weds Michael Jackson

New York, Monday 1
Graceland meets Neverland. At first, publicists for self-proclaimed King of Pop Michael Jackson denied reports in the press that he had married the daughter of, as his fans more succinctly call him, the King. Today, Lisa Marie Presley-Jackson has said that the rumours of a marriage in May in the Dominican Republic are true and that she will "dedicate my life to being his wife". The American royal wedding unites the heiress of Elvis's $100 million Memphis estate, Graceland, with the only singer since the death of her father to come close to matching his success and fame.

Londoners bake as heat wave wilts Europe

London, Tuesday 2
Meteorologists are taking a cool view of the heatwave boiling over on easterly winds from the Continent. "What has happened this summer," said one, "is that we've actually had a summer." Nevertheless, it has been too hot for many, especially in London where 40 people fainted at a Buckingham Palace garden party, and rhinos in the London Zoo had to be rubbed down with moisturising cream. High ozone levels have brought on an asthma epidemic, and pigs have found it too hot to mate. Ice cream and sun tan lotion sellers have made fortunes. Thunderflies are swarming. The forecast: Hot.

UK protests against Bay of Biscay affront

Newlyn, Cornwall, Thursday 4
Britain has sent the HMS *Anglesey*, a fisheries gunboat, to protect British trawlers on tuna-fishing grounds in international waters 400 miles south of Land's End. Twice in the last 24 hours, Spanish trawlers have surrounded Cornish boats and slashed their gear. The Spaniards, who fish with old-fashioned long lines, accuse the Cornish boats of using nets illegal under European Union rules, but the Cornishmen insist their nets, with big gaps to allow dolphins and porpoises through, comply with the rules.

August 1. The years go by, and the Stones rock'n roll on: Mick and Co launch their 12th US tour in Washington.

Six Kurdish MPs face death penalty as key trial opens in Ankara

Ankara, Wednesday 3
At the opening of a trial which could further weaken Turkey's democratic credentials, the prosecution today demanded the death penalty for six Kurdish MPs. Charged with treason, the MPs were stripped of their parliamentary immunity after Prime Minister Tansu Ciller described them as "traitors under the parliament roof". They are accused of acting as the political wing of the PKK, the Kurdish separatist militants. The State Security Court was surrounded by riot police, and the accused were blocked from the view of human rights observers by a wall of policemen.

All the MPs are accused of what the authorities term 'separatist crimes'.

Algerian extremists are seized in France

France, Friday 5
France has arrested 16 Algerian Muslim fundamentalists and plans to deport them. The roundup comes two days after the killing of three French paramilitary gendarmes and two consular officials in the North African country. At least 56 foreigners have been killed in Algeria in the last year, 15 of them French. Paris is urging its allies to clamp down on members of Algeria's Islamic Salvation Front exiled in the West. Interior Minister Charles Pasqua said he would maintain "a high state of vigilance" against the extremists. (→ 26)

Birth defects are new fear of Gulf War vets

Washington, Friday 5
The US Senate Veterans' Affairs Committee heard evidence today that "a wide variety of reproductive toxicants" were present in the Persian Gulf, and that the Pentagon did not do enough to protect the troops. About a year after the war to push Iraq out of Kuwait ended in early 1991, veterans were complaining of a wide variety of ailments: rashes, headaches, nausea, blood clots and more. In the years following, many have had children, and an alarming number of them have been born with birth defects.

Haitian strongman Raoul Cédras says US invasion is inevitable

Port-au-Prince, Saturday 6
General Raoul Cédras, leader of the Haitian military junta, said today it was inevitable that the Americans would mount an invasion to restore to power Jean-Bertrand Aristide, the man he deposed. "It has been decided to invade and we are awaiting this moment," he boasted. "Our soldiers have sworn to defend our country." There would be much bloodshed on both sides, he said, and President Clinton would be to blame. The general may have to wait for his war. Reports from Washington suggest Clinton is too preoccupied with health care reform to invade Haiti until next month. (→ 28)

A well protected General Cédras and his wife tour the streets of Port-au-Prince.

August 4. The royal family and 3,000 well-wishers turned out to wish the Queen Mother a happy 94th birthday.

A 'people's palace' for Queen, MP says

London, Saturday 6
Mo Mowlam, who would be National Heritage Secretary in a Labour government, unveiled plans today for Buckingham Palace and Windsor Castle to be sold off to a body such as the National Trust. The royal family would be moved into a modern "people's palace" built by Britain's top architects, decorated by designers such as Sir Terence Conran and financed by the royals, industry sponsorship and "palace bonds" bought by the public. The new palace, she argues, would help Britain face the future "with a confidence based on reality rather than faded images of past glories."

Helsinki, 7
Solomon Wariso, British 200-metres sprinter, is sent home from the European Athletics Championships for using ephedrine, a banned stimulant.

Bujumbura, 8
At least 15 people are killed in two days of riots after the arrest of Tutsi opposition leader Mathias Hitimana.

Sweden, 10
Bangladeshi writer Taslima Nasrin, under a death threat from Islamic fundamentalists, arrives after fleeing her country.

Kishinev, Moldova, 10
Russia and Moldova agree on a timetable for withdrawal of Russian troops from the former Soviet republic.

Belfast, 11
Sir Hugh Annesley, chief of the RUC, says Britain will reduce the number of troops on patrol in Northern Ireland if the IRA agrees to a ceasefire. (→14)

London, 12
John Paul Getty II pledges £1 million to block the sale of The Three Graces to the California museum established by his late father and keep the sculpture in Britain.

Helsinki, 12
At the European Championships, Sally Gunnell wins the 400-metre hurdles, adding the title to her Olympic, World and Commonwealth honours; Colin Jackson wins the 110-metre hurdles.

United States, 12
Major league baseball strike begins. (→14/9)

Geneva, 13
In an agreement with the US, North Korea says it will freeze its programme to produce plutonium and remain a party to the Nuclear Nonproliferation Treaty.

DEATHS

7. Liu Haisu, Chinese painter and art historian (*16/3/1896).

10. Kay Petre, British rally driver (*1937).

13. Manfred Worner, German politician, civilian head of NATO (*24/9/34).

Castro threatens a new refugee crisis

Washington is afraid that the trickle of boat people, or 'balseros', heading for Florida will turn into a huge flood.

Cuba, Sunday 7
Cuban leader Fidel Castro has threatened to inundate American shores with a tidal wave of boat people. The number of fleeing Cubans has risen dramatically this year; more than 4,000 have entered the US at Key West, as compared to less than 3,000 last year. Castro made his threat after protests on Thursday and Friday, when as many as 10,000 Cubans demonstrated against the regime on the Malecon, Havana's waterfront. The ageing "lider maximo" said that if the US did not "take serious measures to guard their coasts", he would stop blocking the exit of would-be emigrants to the US. Floridians now fear a repeat of the 1980 Mariel boatlift, when 125,000 Cubans, many of whom were freed criminals or mental patients, arrived over a period of several months. A State Department spokesman said, "We will not permit Fidel Castro to dictate our immigration policy." (→24)

Border post opens as tension between Jordan and Israel abates

After 46 years of hostilities, an arid crossing at Arava, near Aqaba, is now open.

Arava, Monday 8
Prime Minister Yitzhak Rabin of Israel and Crown Prince Hassan of Jordan simultaneously cut a white ribbon to open a crossing between their two countries here today. The ceremony, under the benign eye of US Secretary of State Warren Christopher, follows agreements signed in Washington earlier this month by Rabin and King Hussein and signifies the end of 46 years of hostilities. Prince Hassan caught the spirit of the moment, quoting from the Bible in broken Hebrew: "Turning the vale of trouble into the gate of hope."

Tourists will be able to use the crossing. But they must take care; it runs through a minefield.

UK sprinter Christie triumphs in Helsinki

Helsinki, Monday 8
Linford Christie and Steve Backley won gold medals for Britain at the European Athletics Championships here today. Christie, the Olympics champion, stormed home in his cus-

A medal won in just 10.14 seconds.

tomary style in 10.14 seconds to win his third consecutive European 100-metres title. Backley's defence of his javelin title in what is always a keenly contested event was perhaps more remarkable as he has struggled with injury all season. He threw 85.20 metres in the second round and no one could match him. (→ 14)

Hostages are to die, Khmer Rouge claim

Cambodia, Sunday 7
The Khmer Rouge is threatening to kill three Western hostages if their countries continue to supply military aid to the Cambodian government. An American, a Frenchman and an Australian were captured on July 26 in a train ambush. A rebel radio broadcast today said: "If the United States, Australia and France are waging war to kill Cambodians, then Americans, Australians and French will also be killed or wounded." A letter to the Phnom Penh government from the Khmer Rouge also contained an implied threat that the Westerners would be killed if a ransom was not paid. (→ 2/11)

Chechen leader Dudayev mobilises forces

Fighters in the breakaway republic prepare for the arrival of Russian troops.

Grozny, Thursday 11
Fearing military intervention from Russia, General Dzhokar Dudayev, president of the lawless, mountainous republic of Chechenia, today ordered full mobilisation, imposed a state of emergency and stopped Russian TV broadcasts. He also ordered officials to swear an oath on the Koran to Chechenia's independence. "If Russia tries to solve the problem by force," he says, "the ensuing war will make Afghanistan pale into insignificance." President Yeltsin dismisses his fears: "Armed interference is impossible."

National identity card move causes concern

London, Tuesday 9
A government proposal for a new plastic driving licence which could be turned into a "smart" card by the addition of a microchip has brought objections from civil liberties groups who are opposed to the introduction of a national identity card. "The more information a card carries, the more likely it is to be used as an identity card," said Andrew Puddephatt of Liberty.

Much talk, not much good news at international AIDS conference

Pictures of some of the victims of the deadly virus are exhibited in Yokohama.

The prince of ghouls, Peter Cushing, dies

Canterbury, Thursday 11
Peter Cushing, who died of cancer at a hospice here today, was everyone's ideal Frankenstein. With his gaunt face and ability to exude sinister charm, he formed, with Christo-

He was also a true classical actor.

pher Lee and Vincent Price, a distinguished trio of horror film stars. Yet he did not come to horror – which he called fantasy – until he was 45. His early work was mainly in the theatre before he moved to television, where he had a memorable success as Winston Smith in *1984*. He was born on May 26, 1913.

Yokohama, Thursday 11
The 10th International Conference on AIDS, which reached its conclusion here today, heard precious little good news. More than 17 million people have been infected with HIV, with sub-Saharan Africa accounting for 10 million cases. The delegates did hear that taking AZT during the last three months of pregnancy can help reduce the risk that HIV-infected mothers will transmit the virus to their babies. Scientists are also working on developing gene therapy techniques, but practical application is still a long way off. However, these costly treatments will mean little to impoverished nations where the disease is spreading at alarming rates.

United States, 14
A medical journal reports that taking aspirin can help prevent colon cancer.

Budapest, 14
Michael Schumacher wins the Hungarian Grand Prix.

Tulsa, Oklahoma, 14
Zimbabwean golfer Nick Price wins the US PGA Championship.

Helsinki, 14
On the last day of the European Championships, the British team wins the 400-metre relay for a total of six gold medals.

New York, 17
The UN Population Fund says there will be 8.5 billion people in the world by the year 2050.

Lesotho, 17
Four people are killed in riots after King Letsie III dissolves the country's first democratically elected government in 23 years.

Dublin, 18
Martin "The General" Cahill, Ireland's most notorious gangster, is shot to death; the IRA claims responsibility for the "execution".

Kuala Lumpur, 18
Malaysia bans men who "behave like women" from appearing on television, for fear that "weaklings" would lessen industrial productivity.

Sydney, 18
In a move seen as the designation of the heir-apparent to his publishing empire, Rupert Murdoch names his son Lachlan general manager of Queensland Newspapers.

Sri Lanka, 19
Chandrika Kumaratunga takes office as Sri Lanka's first socialist premier in 17 years and proposes "unconditional" talks with the Tamil rebels. (→ 31)

London, 20
German World Cup team-member Jurgen Klinsmann makes his debut in English football, scoring the winning goal in Tottenham's 4-3 season-opening victory over Sheffield.

DEATH

14. Elias Canetti, British author (*25/7/05).

Carlos the Jackal is arrested at last

Paris, Monday 15
Carlos the Jackal, the world's most wanted terrorist, is held under close guard in La Santé prison after being captured in the Sudan in mysterious circumstances over the weekend. Wanted for at least 15 murders in France, he faces a life sentence. Born Illich Ramirez Sanchez, the son of a Stalinist millionaire in Venezuela, he was trained as a terrorist from an early age, becoming the chief hitman in Europe for the Popular Front for the Liberation of Palestine. He achieved notoriety in Paris in 1975 when he shot his way out of an apartment, killing two policemen and wounding a third. His most audacious exploit was the capture of OPEC heaquarters in Vienna at Christmas 1975 and the kidnapping of several oil ministers. However, with the death of his protector, Waddi Hadad of the PFLP, he lost his power base, and despite being

Some of the many faces of the world's most notorious international terrorist.

allowed facilities in East Germany, he found it increasingly difficult to operate as he was made unwelcome by a succession of Arab countries. Syria got rid of him to appease the US. Sudan was his last bolt-hole, and it appears that some sort of deal was done between Sudan and France. Asked how he is, Carlos shrugs and says, "I'm alive." (→ 21)

Peace hopes rising 25 years after British troops came to Belfast

Belfast, Sunday 14
The IRA marked today's 25th anniversary of the deployment of British troops on Belfast's streets by hiding bombs in the panniers of mountain bikes and planting them at the south coast resorts of Bognor and Brighton on Saturday. However, despite this apparent signal that the war of terror will continue, there is still much speculation here that the IRA will declare a ceasefire by the end of the month. Sinn Fein leader Gerry Adams gave a tantalising hint today when he told Republican marchers he was confident the peace process could move towards its goal of a negotiated political settlement. (→ 27)

Prince in Provence for 1944 ceremony

Nice, Sunday 14

Prince Andrew is taking part in celebrations marking the 50th anniversary of Operation Anvil, the Allied landings in the south of France when 400,000 troops, primarily French colonial soldiers, stormed

ashore from 2,000 ships. In two weeks they cleared the whole of the coastal region. Today the prince joined President Mitterrand, Prime Minister Balladur and the heads of 15 former French African colonies on board the carrier *Foch* to review a 33-ship fleet which included seven American and two British vessels.

Nobel great Pauling dies of cancer at 93

Big Sur, California, Friday 19

Linus Pauling, who received Nobel prizes for Peace and for Chemistry, died today at his ranch here. Born on February 28, 1901, the scientist won his first Nobel in 1954 for his research into the force that gives atoms the cohesiveness to form molecules. He also was a pioneer in research into the structure of DNA.

Pauling was an untiring advocate for peace as well, and his work led to McCarthyite accusations of his being a communist sympathiser. The State Department denied him a passport for this reason in 1952. But he continued his activism and led other scientists in a campaign against nuclear testing. In 1962, he was awarded the Peace prize for his work "against all warfare as a means of solving international conflicts".

Hippies and yuppies crowd to giant 'Son of Woodstock' mudbath

Saugerties, New York, Sunday 14

Some 350,000 people got "back to the garden" at Woodstock II this weekend, 25 years after the original "days of peace, love and music". The concert united pot-smoking hippies, portable-phone-toting yuppies, and body-pierced Generation Xers. It rained just like last time, and mudbaths were in. Woodstock '69 veterans Joe Cocker, Santana and Crosby, Stills & Nash shared the stage with youngsters such as James, Nine Inch Nails and Red Hot Chili Peppers. The World Music trend was represented by Senegalese star Youssou N'Dour, and rappers Salt-N-Pepa rocked the mike.

August 19. Queen Elizabeth II officially opens the 15th Commonwealth Games in Victoria, Canada, and the mixed-race South African team get an ovation as they prepare to take part in the games for the first time since 1958.

August
1994

Su	Mo	Tu	We	Th	Fr	Sa
	1	2	3	4	5	6
7	8	9	10	11	12	13
14	15	16	17	18	19	20
21	22	23	24	25	26	27
28	29	30	31			

Coventry, 21
Golfer Colin Montgomerie wins the English Open.

France, 21
Capt Paul Barril, a former member of an elite anti-terrorism unit, says he received instructions in the early 1980s to assassinate Jacques Vergès, the lawyer now defending international terrorist Carlos, and that President Mitterrand was aware of his mission.

Somalia, 22
Seven Indian UN soldiers are killed and nine wounded in an attack by Somali militiamen.

Moscow, 22
After a rash of arrests of plutonium smugglers in Germany, Moscow and Bonn agree to work together to prevent smuggling of nuclear materials from Russia.

Victoria, Canada, 23
Annika Reeder, 14, becomes England's youngest ever Commonwealth Games gold medalist, winning the gymnastic floor exercises.

Islamabad, 24
Nawaz Sharif, former prime minister of Pakistan, says his country possesses the atomic bomb; his assertion is promptly denied by the government.

London, 25
Diane Modahl, 800-metres champion, and Paul Edwards, a shot putter, are flown home from the Commonwealth Games after positive drug tests.

Algeria, 26
The hardline Armed Islamic Group announces the formation of an alternative government.

Hanoi, 26
Tomiichi Murayama ends his visit to Vietnam, the first by a Japanese prime minister; he promises aid and says Vietnam should join ASEAN.

Moscow, 26
Newsweek magazine says the Russian mafia has threatened its staff and demanded to be paid for "protection".

Belfast, 27
The Northern Ireland Office says that British law provides for a change in the status of Ulster if a majority of the population wants it. (→ 31)

Another mass exodus feared as France ends Rwanda operation

The French military intervention has done little to ease the refugees' plight.

Rwanda, Sunday 21
As the French Operation Turquoise comes to an end today, thousands of Hutu are trying to leave the country in fear of retaliation by the Tutsi-dominated Rwanda Patriotic Front, which deposed the former Hutu government earlier this summer. UN forces are to take over in the humanitarian protection zone in the southwest, and the RPF has promised not to invade. But assurances by UN officials and relief workers that the Hutu are safe has not dissuaded large numbers of them from trying to flee to Zaire. The Zairian town of Bukavu is already teeming with 100,000 refugees, and a repeat of the Goma disaster is feared.

Mexico votes to stick with PRI as Zedillo wins presidential election

Mexico, Monday 22
Showing a desire for stability after a politically turbulent year, Mexicans today elected the ruling Institutional Revolutionary Party candidate, Ernesto Zedillo Ponce de Leon, as their next president. Zedillo was picked by his party to run after his successor was assassinated in March. The country has also been shaken by a peasant revolt in the state of Chiapas and by turmoil in the stock market. Zedillo won 50% of the vote, the conservative Diego Fernandez de Cevallos was second with 27%, and the leftist candidate Cuauhtemoc Cardenas Solorzano, the only one with the support of the rebel Zapatistas, pulled in 17%.

The ruling party's candidate benefitted from the voters' desire for stability.

Princess Diana embroiled in furore over mystery telephone calls

Oliver Hoare complained to the police after a spate of anonymous phone calls.

London, Monday 22
The Princess of Wales is considering legal action over allegations that she made a series of nuisance telephone calls to a married friend, art dealer Oliver Hoare, who complained to the police.

MPs are calling for a Scotland Yard investigation into the leaking of details of the inquiry into the calls which were traced to telephones used by the princess. She has gone public, giving an interview to the *Daily Mail* in which she denies making the calls and provides details of her diary to disprove the allegations. She says: "Somewhere, someone is going to make out that I am mad."

Bill Clinton's $30 billion anti-crime bill is approved by Congress

The bill outlaws 19 types of semi-automatic assault weapons such as these.

Washington, Thursday 25
In an election year, President Clinton was able to pull enough Republicans away from their party line to pass his crime bill. Voters see the issue as one of the most pressing facing America. The Senate voted 61-38 today to approve the $30.2 billion bill. $13.4 billion will go to law enforcement, putting 100,000 new police on the streets and paying for research into DNA fingerprinting. Prevention programmes, the part of the bill to which Republicans object, will cost $6.9 billion. $9.9 billion will go to building prisons. The bill also bans a wide variety of assault weapons, such as AK-47s, Uzi pistols and grenade launchers.

US is unable to stem the tide of 'balseros'

Washington, Wednesday 24
Cubans are taking to the Strait of Florida in rickety boats, rafts and even inner tubes by the thousands to leave their country for the US. More than 8,700 Cubans have been picked up by the Coast Guard since Friday, when President Clinton announced that he was ending the 28-year-old policy of automatically granting political asylum to Cuban emigrants. Washington today moved to expand its facilities at Guantanamo Bay to hold 40,000 refugees and is sending television and radio broadcasts to Cuba telling would-be "balseros" that they should stay home. (9/9)

Serbs in Bosnia vote against peace plan

Pale, Bosnia, Saturday 27
Bosnian Serbs are voting this weekend on whether or not to accept the latest international peace plan and they are giving the plan an emphatic thumbs down. They are refusing to have anything to do with a plan which involves them giving up territory they have won by force of arms. In doing so they are further humiliating the Serbian leader Slobodan Milosevic. He may cut them adrift in revenge but, fiercely nationalistic, they remain defiant. (→ 7/9)

Storm clouds hang over 'Sunset Boulevard'

London, Friday 26
Sir Andrew Lloyd Webber is considering issuing a counter-writ against Faye Dunaway, who is suing him after being sacked from the Los Angeles production of the musical *Sunset Boulevard* because her singing "was not up to standard". The actress, who is asking for more than $6 million, said: "I am the last in a long line of artists who have come to this man's productions in good faith and suffered great personal and professional injury at his hands." Sir Andrew considers this "insulting, damaging and defamatory".

Faye Dunaway is suing Andrew Lloyd Webber for a whopping $6 million.

August 26. A sea of banners flows down the Champs Elysées as tens of thousands of Parisians and tourists celebrate the 50th anniversary of the liberation of the city by General Philippe Leclerc's 2nd Armoured Division.

August

1994

Su	Mo	Tu	We	Th	Fr	Sa
	1	2	3	4	5	6
7	8	9	10	11	12	13
14	15	16	17	18	19	20
21	22	23	24	25	26	27
28	29	30	31			

Jericho, 28
The Israeli mayor officially hands over administrative authority to the new Palestinian council.

Dusseldorf, 28
Scottish golfer Colin Montgomerie wins the German Open.

Port-au-Prince, 28
Jean-Marie Vincent, a prominent pro-Aristide Roman Catholic priest, is killed by suspected army gunmen. (→ 1/9)

Russia, 28
Russia is withdrawing the kopek, 290 years after its introduction; the coin is worth one hundredth of a ruble or three millionths of one pence.

South Korea, 29
Samsung says it has developed a computer chip with memory capability of 256 megabits – enough to hold the equivalent of 2,000 newspaper pages; production should begin in 1997.

United States, 29
US defence contractors Lockheed and Martin Marietta announce their merger.

Beijing, 31
The Chinese parliament votes to disband Hong Kong's legislature and the colony's other elected institutions when China takes over in 1997.

Germany, 31
The last Russian troops leave the country; withdrawals are completed in Latvia and Estonia as well.

Sri Lanka, 31
In a move toward making peace with the Tamil Tigers, Prime Minister Kumaratunga lifts the economic embargo on areas held by the rebels.

London, 31
The government announces that Ebbsfleet, Kent, will be the site for one of two international stations on the high-speed rail link from London to the Channel Tunnel.

Tokyo, 31
Japan says its £280 million Engineering Test Satellite 6 will become space junk; complications have forced the space agency to give up trying to place it in proper orbit.

Michael Schumacher's disqualification gives victory to Damon Hill

Spa-Francorchamps, Sunday 28
Michael Schumacher ran into more trouble yesterday when he was disqualified from the Belgian Grand Prix five hours after crossing the winning line. The stewards found that the speed-limiting wooden plank fitted to his Benetton Ford was thinner than the regulations stipulate. The victory now goes to Damon Hill, and Schumacher's seemingly impregnable lead in the driver's championship is reduced from 35 to 21 points. As he is facing a two-race ban for ignoring a black flag, he now becomes vulnerable.

A dejected Hill (left) stands on the podium prior to the race officials' verdict.

Clean-cut, naive 'Forrest Gump' is surprise box-office hit in US

United States, Wednesday 31
Summer is a big season for films here, with the hot weather drawing Americans into the dark, air-conditioned cinemas. An estimated $2.2 billion (£1.5 billion) in box-office receipts have been raked in. One of the surprise blockbusters has been *Forrest Gump*, which was released in July and has made $222 million. The title character, a good-hearted simpleton who encounters success at every turn, has enchanted moviegoers. The top money-earner, Disney's *The Lion King*, has pulled in $257 million since mid-June. The animated feature is the story of a lion-cub prince exiled by an evil uncle after the death of his father.

Aug. 29. Japan's new Kansai international airport, costing £10 billion and built on a 511-hectare man-made island.

US Navy to disband its elite dolphin unit

San Diego, Wednesday 31
Military cutbacks have affected an elite force of the US Navy: 30 of a 100-strong team of diving experts will be made redundant. The team is composed of dolphins, which performed dangerous search and demolition missions and served as guards for US ships anchored in seas across the globe. The dolphins are going to new homes in amusement centres, aquariums and parks; the Navy says the tamed mammals would not be able to survive in the wild.

Lindsay Anderson, iconoclast director, dies

London, Tuesday 30
Lindsay Anderson (*17/4/23), the major-general's son who rampaged like a rogue elephant through London's often precious film and theatre world, died today of a heart attack in France. Echoes of his military family upbringing sounded through his subversive film *If...*, a story of school life in which discontent turns into bloody rebellion. His other films, among them *This Sporting Life* and *Oh Lucky Man*, were equally iconoclastic. Often mauled by the critics, he remained faithful to his anarchical talent.

Japan's 'sex slaves' to get compensation

Tokyo, Wednesday 31
The Japanese government today announced plans to compensate symbolically the "comfort women" of Korea, the Philippines and other countries who were forced into sexual slavery by Japanese troops in World War II. The 10-year, £650 million programme will pay for vocational centres for women in several Asian countries and for research on the war. Critics say the plan does not go far enough and call for direct compensation for the war victims.

Shakespeare's Globe Theatre slowly takes shape on South Bank

London, August
The dream of the late American actor Sam Wanamaker is finally being realised. Workers are labouring in this summer's stifling heat to finish the reconstruction of the Globe Theatre, where the comedies and tragedies of William Shakespeare were first performed. Wanamaker initiated the project in the early seventies, but the building work, just a few dozen yards away from the original site, did not begin until five years ago. The main oak structure is now up, and the open-air theatre should have its first season next year. A Shakespeare museum and educational centre will also be included in the project.

Computer chess loss for Garri Kasparov

London, Wednesday 31
A stunned Garri Kasparov was eliminated by a computer today from the Intel Speed Chess Grand Prix held in the City of London. The world champion, playing with the advantage of the white pieces, started confidently, but the lightning speed of the Genius 2 software in his opponent, a Pentium computer, proved too much for him. The 300 spectators watching the game on a giant video screen were astonished as he was outplayed in the first game. In the second game he was forced to offer a draw and was thus out of the competition.

Spend, spend, spend for Sunday shoppers

London, Monday 29
People throughout Britain responded enthusiastically to the Sunday Trading Act, which came into effect yesterday, and turned out in their thousands to take advantage of the first legal Sunday openings in England and Wales. They spent millions of pounds. Under the Act large stores can open for up to six hours and small shops for as long as they wish. At the Metro-Centre in Gateshead, England's biggest indoor shopping complex, where the landlords are the Church commissioners, a service with hymns and Bible readings was held to provide a touch of traditional Sunday to 90,000 shoppers who spent an average of £57 each.

August 31. VW unveils the Polo, its new mass-market contender, with a 1,300 or 1,600cc four-cylinder engine.

Historic crossroads reached in Ulster
Northern Ireland's quarter century of violence and hate

14/8/69: The first British troops are deployed in Belfast and Londonderry.

7/9/71: Another victim of the troubles is buried as the death toll reaches 100.

30/1/72: Two of the 13 civilians killed in the Bogside on 'Bloody Sunday'.

27/8/79: Lord Mountbatten is killed when an IRA bomb destroys his boat.

12/10/84: Margaret Thatcher survives an IRA bomb attack in Brighton.

19/3/88: One of two British soldiers beaten to death by a mob in West Belfast.

as an IRA ceasefire goes into effect
Republican truce sparks an upsurge of hopes for peace

Sinn Fein's Martin McGuinness.

The men of violence wait and see.

How will the Rev Ian Paisley react?

Belfast, Wednesday 31

After a quarter century of bombing and killing and the deaths of more than 3,000 people, the IRA has announced a "complete cessation of military operations", and the way now seems open to a political settlement of this savage sectarian conflict. Gerry Adams, president of Sinn Fein, who persuaded the IRA hardliners to accept the Downing Street Declaration, said: "We have taken a great step by removing the Republican gun from Irish politics." Tonight there are triumphant celebrations in the Catholic areas of Belfast and Londonderry.

However, one major problem has surfaced immediately. The IRA document speaks of a "cessation" of military operations but does not use the word "permanent", a condition laid down in the declaration as a prerequisite for Sinn Fein to join talks on the future of Northern Ireland. The British Government has demanded clarification from the IRA, and Prime Minister John Major said tonight: "We need to be sure that the cessation of violence isn't temporary; that it isn't for one week or one month, but a permanent cessation of violence." Irish Prime Minister Albert Reynolds, who has done so much to bring about peace, has telephoned Major to reassure him that although the word "permanent" was not in the statement, other phrases showed the Republican movement was now committed to a democratic peace process. "As far as we are concerned the long nightmare is over," he said.

The reaction of the Protestant community is less ecstatic. Ian Paisley said the IRA's "war machine" could be turned on at any time, and there was much scepticism about the worth of the IRA's word. Major must convince the Loyalists that they have not been sold out in some secret deal. If he can do that and reassure them they will remain part of the United Kingdom as long as a majority wishes, then peace will stand a chance. As the prime minister said tonight: "We are beyond the beginning, but we are not yet in sight of the end." (→8/9)

An unusual and uneasy calm now reigns in the mean steets of Londonderry.

Today's unilateral IRA ceasefire brings renewed hope for the children of Ulster.

Politicians in Westminster and Dublin await the response of Loyalist leaders.

1994

Su	Mo	Tu	We	Th	Fr	Sa
				1	2	3
4	5	6	7	8	9	10
11	12	13	14	15	16	17
18	19	20	21	22	23	24
25	26	27	28	29	30	

Washington, 1
Pentagon experts estimate that a US invasion of Haiti would cost at least $427 million. (→19)

Bordeaux, 2
Miguel Indurain of Spain breaks Chris Boardman's world one-hour cycling record, covering 53.04 kilometres.

Moscow, 3
Presidents Boris Yeltsin of Russia and Jiang Zemin of China agree never again to aim nuclear missiles at each other's country.

Ontario, 4
A 26-year-old woman whose parachute malfunctions plummets 10,000 feet into a marsh but suffers only minor bruises.

Germany, 5
According to an opinion poll, only 15% of the German population is anti-Semitic, a postwar low.

Moscow, 5
First Deputy Foreign Minister Anatoli Adamishin is appointed Russian ambassador to Britain.

Moscow, 6
A government commission reports that Princess Anastasia was indeed murdered along with her family, including her father Tsar Nicholas II, by the Bolsheviks in 1918.

Kuala Lumpur, 7
Malaysia lifts a seven-month ban on awarding government contracts to British firms.

London, 7
Foreign Secretary Douglas Hurd says British peacekeepers will be pulled out of Bosnia if the United Nations embargo on arms to Bosnian forces is lifted. (→22)

London, 9
John Major announces a "national partnership against the criminal" and calls for stiffer penalties to combat the "yob culture".

DEATHS

3. Billy Wright, former England football captain (*6/2/24).

6. James Clavell, British author (*10/10/24).

7. Terence Young, British film director (*20/6/15).

Much loved comedian Roy Castle dies after fight against cancer

Buckinghamshire, Friday 2
Roy Castle, the entertainer, lost his two-and-a-half-year struggle against cancer today. A great favourite in the music halls and on television, where he hosted *The Record Breakers*, which ran for over a decade, he won a host of new admirers by the way he battled with his illness. In a series of gruelling tours, often taking the stage suffering from the side-effects of his treatment, he raised millions of pounds to found an international cancer centre in Liverpool. His wife, Fiona, who was with him when he died, said that she wanted him remembered with happiness: "No flowers, no fuss, no mourning, just lots of joy." He was born at Scholes, North Yorkshire, on August 31, 1932.

Texas is abuzz with tales of 'killer' bees

Georgetown, Texas, Saturday 3
A furious swarm of 75,000 Africanised honey bees attacked two men here and then swarmed the ambulance taking them to hospital today. This town near Austin is the most northern site of a "killer" bee attack. The bees are descendants of African bees imported to Brazil for breeding in 1957. Since then, the species has been heading north. The bees are dangerous not because of their venom but because of their habit of attacking in gigantic swarms.

Harvest of titles for Chinese swim team

Rome, Monday 5
The Chinese women's team were the stars of the opening day of the World Swimming Championships here today, taking all three women's gold medals. Le Jingyi became the first Chinese to break the 100-metre freestyle record, with a time of 54.01 seconds. Lu Bin set a championship record, winning the 800-metre freestyle relay at 7:59.96. Dai Guohong completed the sweep by taking the gold medal in the women's 400-metre medley.

Major opposes plan for a two-tier Europe

Leiden, Holland, Wednesday 7
John Major, delivering the William and Mary Lecture at Leiden University tonight, warned that French and German proposals for an elite grouping within the EU were a recipe for disaster. "I recoil from ideas for a Union in which some would be more equal than others," he said. "There is not, and should never be, an exclusive hard core either of countries or of policies. ... The way the Union develops should be acceptable to all member states."

September 3. The clans have gathered at Braemar once again to compete in the traditional Highland Games.

USAF responsible for 1947 UFO mystery

Washington, Thursday 8

For decades, UFO spotters have claimed that the US government was hiding information about the 1947 crash of a mysterious craft in the New Mexico desert. Pictures of the wreckage taken by local people fueled reports that the craft was a spaceship and that bodies of aliens recovered in the crash were being studied by military scientists. The Air Force released a report today explaining that what they hurried to spirit away from the crash site was a balloon used to monitor Soviet nuclear tests. Project Mogul detected the detonation of the first Soviet nuclear bomb in 1949 but was ended the next year.

Loyalists pose six ceasefire demands

A furious Ian Paisley leaves Downing Street after his row with John Major.

London, Thursday 8

The Irish peace initiative is rushing along a dangerous road at a furious pace. On Tuesday, only six days after the IRA declared a ceasefire, Irish Prime Minister Albert Reynolds met Sinn Fein President Gerry Adams in Dublin. On the same day, John Major threw Ian Paisley out of his office after the hardline unionist refused to accept his word that he had not made a secret deal with the IRA. And today, the Protestant paramilitaries tabled a list of demands including a guarantee on the constitutional position of Northern Ireland within the United Kingdom that would have to be met before they could make "a meaningful contribution to peace". (→ 12)

Right royal row over full-frontal Charles

London, Wednesday 7

Buckingham Palace is considering taking legal action against *Bild* and *Paris Match* for publishing full frontal photographs of the Prince of Wales in the nude. The grainy photographs were taken with a long lens through the window of his bedroom in a chateau where he was holidaying in the south of France. The prince's press secretary, Allan Percival, said: "We think it is completely unjustifiable for anybody to suffer this sort of intrusion."

Cuba and US reach accord aimed at halting the refugee exodus

A US Navy vessel takes Cuban refugees to the American base at Guantanamo.

Washington, Friday 9

The Clinton administration and the government of Fidel Castro have reached an agreement on stopping the exodus of Cubans to the United States. For the last month, about 1,000 Cubans a day have tried to cross the Strait of Florida by boat. Washington has agreed to increase the number of Cubans allowed to enter the US legally to 20,000 a year, up from 3,000, but the "balseros" picked up at sea will not be allowed immediate entry to the US. Havana will use "mainly persuasive measures" to stop Cubans leaving.

Sept. 8. As John Major, Helmut Kohl and François Mitterrand look on, the last Allied soldiers bid farewell after spending nearly 50 years in Berlin.

Sept. 10. On his first foreign visit in a year, Pope John Paul II delivers a message of hope in Zagreb, the capital of predominantly Catholic Croatia.

September

1994

Su	Mo	Tu	We	Th	Fr	Sa
				1	2	3
4	5	6	7	8	9	10
11	12	13	14	15	16	17
18	19	20	21	22	23	24
25	26	27	28	29	30	

Monza, 11
Damon Hill wins the Italian Grand Prix.

New York, 11
Unseeded Andre Agassi defeats Michael Stich of Germany 6-1, 7-6 (7-5), 7-5 to win the US Open; in the women's final, Arantxa Sanchez beats Steffi Graf 1-6, 7-6 (7-3), 6-4.

Dublin, 12
A UVF bomb explodes on a train, injuring two people. (→ 16)

Venice, 12
Aiqing wansui, by Taiwanese director Tsai Ming-Liang, and *Before the Rain*, by Macedonian director Milcho Manchevski, jointly win the Golden Lion at the Venice Film Festival.

London, 12
The Bank of England raises its key interest rate to 5.75%, the first such increase since 1989.

Washington, 12
A former US treasurer, Catalina Villapando, whose signature once appeared on every dollar bill, is sentenced to four months in jail for tax evasion.

Hamburg, 13
Municipal authorities suspend 27 police officers accused of beating foreigners.

New York, 14
Due to a month-long strike by players, team owners call off the entire baseball season; this means that there will be no World Series for the first time since 1904.

Ramsgate, 14
Six people are killed when a walkway to a ferry collapses.

Washington, 14
US scientists announce they have isolated the gene that causes the inherited form of breast cancer.

Alaska, 16
A court orders Exxon to pay $5 billion in damages to victims of the 1989 *Exxon Valdez* oil spill.

DEATHS

12. Tom Ewell, American comedy actor (*29/4/09).

17. Sir Karl Popper, British philosopher (*28/7/02).

Separatist Parizeau wins vote in Quebec

Quebec, Monday 12
The separatist Parti Quebecois has, as expected, won Quebec's provincial elections but not by the predicted thumping majority. Its share of the vote was 44.7%, while the Liberals, who want to remain in a united Canada, got 44.3%. The results confirmed opinion poll findings that the people wanted a new government, but only a hard core want a new country. Nevertheless, the separatists' leader, Jacques Parizeau, remains confident that he will win a referendum on taking Quebec out of Canada. He promises to hold the poll next year.

Mitterrand explains past in Vichy France

Paris, Monday 12
President Mitterrand appeared on television tonight to reassert his authority and quiet the storm caused by a recent book detailing his activities as a loyal servant of Vichy and Marshal Pétain during the war. Looking gaunt from his treatment for cancer, he started hesitantly but grew confident as the interview progressed, and he vigorously defended his service to the collaborationist state and his long friendship with René Bousquet, the Vichy police chief who sent thousands of French Jews to Nazi death camps.

Sept. 11. Jessica Tandy (*7/6/09), star of *Driving Miss Daisy*, dies.

Man dies in kamikaze White House attack

Washington, Monday 12
A single-engine Cessna 150 airplane penetrated the US capital's no-flight zone at 1:45 this morning, flew in low and crash-landed on the White House South Lawn, 50 feet away from the presidential residence. The plane came to rest against a wall just under the president's second-floor bedroom window. The Secret Service said that the pilot, who died in the crash, was mentally ill and they had no suspicions of the incident being a terrorist attack. (→ 29/10)

Cairo conference on world population crisis

Cairo, Tuesday 13
Against a background of disputes about abortion, contraception and extra-marital sex, the United Nations conference on population ended here today with a 20-year plan to limit the world's population, promote the status of women and preserve the environment. The plan was agreed by consensus; Latin American and Muslim countries expressed formal reservations, while the Vatican said it would join the consensus on some aspects of the programme, but not others, particularly those linked to abortion.

Despite these reservations, Nafis Sadik, head of the UN's Population Fund, said the conference was "an outstanding success".

Sept. 11. A replica Vickers Vimy bomber takes off from the Farnborough Air Show to try to re-create the first Vimy flight to Australia 75 years ago.

'Discovery' astronauts float free in space

Colonel Mark Lee tries out the revolutionary £4 million space pack in orbit.

Houston, Friday 16
Colonel Mark Lee took the first untethered space walk in a decade to test a new NASA jet pack today. He was accompanied on the space walk by Colonel Carl Meade, who put his partner through some astral acrobatics, spinning Lee head over heels.

The jet pack, which cost £4 million to develop, was designed as a safety measure for the construction of a planned space station, codenamed Alpha, due to begin in 1997.

The 83-pound pack uses 24 nitrogen-gas thrusters, which propel the astronaut at a rate of six inches a second. If the umbilical cord to the station is broken, the space-walker will be able to return to safety on his own.

"This thing works like a champ," said Lee. The only hitch was in recharging the pack with nitrogen gas. The pack had to be refilled several times, and this took longer than expected because a connecting hose had to be emptied.

Sept. 15. Heaven on earth: Alain Bernardin (*1916), founder of the Crazy Horse Saloon, a Paris nightlife landmark since 1951, commits suicide.

Pamela Harriman sued in family dispute

The US ambassador to France is now facing a massive $30 million lawsuit.

New York, Friday 16
Pamela Harriman, daughter-in-law of Winston Churchill and the US ambassador to France, is being sued by the two daughters of her late husband Averell, a New York governor and ambassador to London and Moscow. They say she squandered their $30 million trust fund in risky investments. Harriman was first married to Randolph Churchill and then to theatrical producer Leland Hayward. Also named in the suit are the trustees appointed by Harriman before his death, two high-powered Washington lawyers, Clark Clifford and Paul Warnke, who were in Lyndon Johnson's Defence department.

Major promises a poll on Ulster's future

Belfast, Friday 16
John Major flew here tonight to "talk directly" to the people of Northern Ireland. He performed a fine balancing act, lifting the broadcasting ban on Sinn Fein and promising the people of the province a referendum on their future. He guaranteed to put the outcome of any talks between London, Dublin and the political parties directly to the people. Telling them not to be tricked by "siren voices", he said: "The referendum means that it will be your choice whether to accept the outcome. My commitment means that no one can go behind your backs. Not today. Not tomorrow. Not at any time. It will be for you to decide." (→ 27)

Heroes of Arnhem bloodbath remembered

Arnhem, Saturday 17
Thousands of Dutch people braved rain and driving winds today to give their thanks to survivors of the "Red Devils" who dropped here 50 years ago in the gallant but doomed attempt to take "The Bridge Too Far". There was enthusiastic applause as the veterans marched past, but the old soldiers were greatly disappointed because the bad weather meant that it was too dangerous for 48 of them – average age 74 – to re-enact their jump in the presence of Prince Charles. Nothing, however, could dampen the gratitude of the Dutch, who saw Operation Market Garden as the first sign that they would be liberated.

September
1994

Su	Mo	Tu	We	Th	Fr	Sa
				1	2	3
4	5	6	7	8	9	10
11	12	13	14	15	16	17
18	19	20	21	22	23	24
25	26	27	28	29	30	

Hong Kong, 18
In the colony's first fully democratic election, democratic parties take 106 of the 346 district board seats at stake; pro-China parties take 37 and pro-business groups 30.

Woburn, 18
Golfer Ian Woosnam wins the Dunhill Masters.

Sweden, 18
The Social Democrats, in opposition for the last three years, win general elections.

Denmark, 21
The Social Democrats lose some ground in the general elections but remain the strongest party.

Bosnia, 22
NATO jet fighters bomb a Serbian tank near Sarajevo in retaliation for a Serb attack on a UN tank. (→ 6/10)

Cambridgeshire, 22
Semtex high explosive and three detonators are found in Whitemore prison, where five IRA terrorists are held.

Humberside, 22
Rebecca Hewison, the oldest person in Britain, dies; she would have been 113 on October 10.

Turkey, 23
Turkey begins a major infantry and air assault against a Kurdish guerrilla stronghold in the eastern province of Tunceli.

London, 24
Lennox Lewis, the British World Boxing Council's heavyweight champion, is knocked out by American Oliver McCall in the second round.

DEATHS

18. Kenneth Masterson, OBE, Deputy Chief Constable of the RUC (*17/6/46).

18. Vitas Gerulaitis, American tennis player (*26/7/54).

18. Franco Moschino, Italian fashion designer (*27/2/50).

20. Jule Styne, American composer (*31/12/05).

23. Madeleine Renaud, French actress (*21/2/00).

24. Sir David Napley, British solicitor (*25/7/15).

US seizes Haiti without firing a shot

Haiti, Monday 19
American soldiers arrived in Haiti today and did not fire a shot. As the announcements from loudspeakers in army helicopters flying over Port-au-Prince put it: "We're not at war. We're here to restore democracy and supply humanitarian aid."

Haitian and US troops have been spared a bloody invasion due to an 11th-hour agreement in which the junta's leader, Raoul Cédras, promised to step down. The agreement was brokered by a team led by former President Jimmy Carter and including General Colin Powell and Senator Sam Nunn. Clinton sent the team in on Saturday with instructions to determine the "modalities" of the junta's departure and be out by noon Sunday. But negotiations dragged on well past 1:00pm, at which time the president gave the invasion order. Calls and faxes flew between Port-au-Prince and Washington all afternoon, and at 6:45pm, 61 planes carrying invasion troops left the US. These troops were called back at 8:00 when Clinton agreed to Carter's deal: Cédras would resign by October 15, and his army would cooperate with the US military mission, which arrived today. (→ 30)

Sept. 18. Jean Simmons receives a BFI Fellowship in recognition of her long and distinguished career.

Football legend Lineker retires from game

London, Wednesday 21
Gary Lineker, the former England captain now playing in Japan for the Grampus Eight, announced his decision to retire today as soon as the Japanese season ends. Injuries have finally defeated the 33-year-old striker, who scored 48 goals for his country in 80 internationals and, never booked, is one of the most respected men in soccer. His international career came to a controversial end when England manager Graham Taylor substituted him in the game against Sweden in the European Championship finals two years ago. Lineker will not go into management, instead he will develop his career as a media pundit.

Paddy Ashdown calls for links with Labour

Brighton, Thursday 22

Paddy Ashdown put his political life on the line today when he urged his party to make "common cause" with Labour at the next general election. Winding up a rebellious Liberal Democrat conference here, he argued that an injection of Lib Dem ideas could ensure that a Labour government would not be just "candyfloss visions and candystick promises" but a confident, reforming administration. Tory reaction came from party chairman Jeremy Hanley: "Your party looks like Labour, sounds like Labour, acts like Labour. The only difference is that it is even more incoherent."

'Missing link' fossils are found in Ethiopia

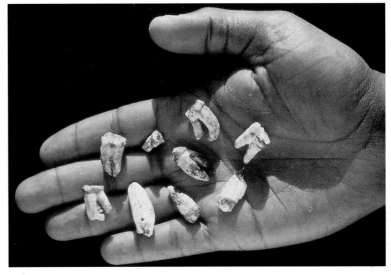

Addis Ababa, Thursday 22

Fossils of a previously unknown human ancestor which could very well be the "missing link" between apes and humans have been found in the Middle Awash region of Ethiopia. At a news conference here today, anthropologist Berhane Asfaw described the individual, whose species has been named *Australopithecus ramidus*, as being between 20 and 30 years old and 4 feet 4 inches tall. *A. ramidus* lived about 4.5 million years ago, about half-a-million years before *A. afarensis*, the species to which the famous Lucy belonged. The fossils of the two species were found about 50 miles apart.

'Cricket nut' John Major visits South Africa

Pretoria, Thursday 22

John Major, whose idea of heaven is a permanent cricket match, bowled South Africa's Sports Minister, Steve Tshwete, first ball yesterday on a rubbish tip converted into a sports arena by British government aid. His three-day visit to South Africa, accompanied by businessmen and sports stars, is judged a success here despite Margaret Thatcher's unhelpful speech in India in which she told businessmen that South Africa still has potential for violent instability. Lady Thatcher later wished Major's mission well.

Thousands flee plague outbreak in India

Surat, India, Saturday 24

Pneumonic plague has struck this western Indian city, and some 300,000 people have fled amid scenes of panic at bus and railway stations. The death toll here, where public buildings have been ordered to be closed, is put at 100. The fear is that the fleeing people will carry the disease to other parts of the country. Health services in Bombay, 100 miles to the south, have been alerted and hospitals are setting up isolation units. The first plague outbreak in Gujurat state in 20 years has caught authorities unprepared.

Su	Mo	Tu	We	Th	Fr	Sa
				1	2	3
4	5	6	7	8	9	10
11	12	13	14	15	16	17
18	19	20	21	22	23	24
25	26	27	28	29	30	

Estoril, 25
Damon Hill wins the Portuguese Grand Prix.

Switzerland, 25
Voters approve laws making racial discrimination, racist propaganda and denying the existence of the Holocaust illegal.

Brussels, 26
The member nations of NATO agree to appoint Belgian Foreign Minister Willy Claes Secretary-General.

France, 27
Californian Chad Hunderby swims the English Channel in the record time of 7 hours, 17 minutes.

Britain, 27
The government reports that crime fell by 5.5% last year, but violent crime and sex offences rose.

Tokyo, 27
Japan formally declares its candidacy for a seat on the UN Security Council.

Washington, 28
Presidents Clinton and Yeltsin agree to speed up dismantling of Russian and US nuclear arsenals and to cooperate more closely on economic and security matters. (→ 30)

Mexico City, 28
Jose Francisco Ruiz Massieu, head of the ruling Party of Institutional Revolution's parliamentary group, is assassinated.

Shannon, Eire, 30
Prime Minister Reynolds waits to meet Boris Yeltsin when his plane lands at the airport; the Russian president never gets off the plane and says on his arrival in Moscow that his aides failed to wake him from a nap.

Washington, 30
The World Health Organization says that polio has been eradicated in the Western hemisphere.

DEATHS

26. Jessie Kesson, Scottish novelist (*28/10/16).

26. Rex Morefoot, BBC broadcaster (*28/1/21).

27. Harry Saltzman, Canadian film producer (*27/10/15).

Boris Yeltsin, John Major agree to focus on closer UK-Russia ties

The leaders and their wives enjoyed a quick drink in a Buckinghamshire pub.

London, Sunday 25
John Major and Boris Yeltsin have spent a country weekend at Chequers with a pub lunch, casual clothes and long walks and today announced themselves very pleased with the results. "We have had a meeting of an entirely different kind," said Major. "It was useful and it was enjoyable, and I believe it reflects the relationship that exists between the United Kingdom and Russia." A beaming Yeltsin agreed: "I consider we have never had such wonderful relations as exist now between Great Britain and Russia." Among the things they discussed over their beer and stilton cheese were a way out of the Bosnian morass and the Queen's forthcoming visit to Russia. (→ 28)

OJ death trial opens amid a media frenzy

The Simpsons: Nicole, OJ and kids.

Los Angeles, Monday 26
The courthouse here is swarming with reporters from newspapers, magazines and television news shows from all over the world.

Today begins the process of selecting a jury for the trial of the most famous American ever to be accused of murder, O J Simpson. Judge Lance Ito will question about 1,000 prospective jurors taken from the list of drivers and registered voters in LA County. The process could take from three to six weeks, and the trial itself could go on at least until February of next year.

Long rail strike ends

London, Tuesday 27
The four-month series of rail strikes which has so frustrated commuters ended last night after more than 60 hours of talks over seven days between negotiators for Railtrack and the Rail, Maritime and Transport Union. A package of measures dealing with pay, restructuring and productivity has now been agreed. The strike, over payments to signalmen for "past efficiency gains", has cost millions of pounds and has always seemed unnecessary and neanderthal to the baffled public.

A gift of life for Italy

Italy, Thursday 29
An American family on holiday – Reginald and Margaret Green and their two children, Nicholas and Eleanor – were driving in southern Italy today when they were attacked by highway bandits. As the Greens sped away in an attempt to escape, the bandits opened fire. Nicholas, 7, was shot in the head and died. The Greens, though wracked by sorrow, chose to do a magnanimous thing: They informed the hospital they wished to donate their son's organs to Italians in need of transplants.

September 29. Back from the deep: a well preserved sink recovered from the wreck of the *Titanic* in mid-Atlantic is one of the 3,600 objects from the ill-fated liner exhibited at the National Maritime Museum in Greenwich.

900 people are killed in Baltic Sea ferry tragedy

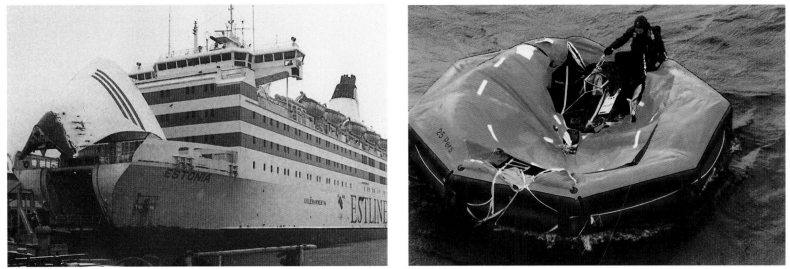

While the massive rescue operation continues (right), maritime experts say that faulty seals on the Estonia's huge bow doors could be the cause of the disaster.

Stockholm, Wednesday 28
The roll-on, roll-off ferry *Estonia* sank in heavy weather in the Baltic early this morning, going down in minutes with a terrible loss of life. It is feared that as many as 900 people have died. Survivors speak of water pouring through the bow doors before the 15,567-ton ferry capsized. An SOS signal sent at 12:20am said "Mayday. Heavy list, 20 degrees, 30 degrees. Blackout." Five minutes later another message said: "We are sinking, the engines have stopped."

Nothing more was heard from the stricken ship. She went down in 300 feet of bitterly cold water. There are 141 confirmed survivors out of more than 1,000 passengers and crew, and there is no hope for anyone else. The sinking of the *Estonia*, with its frightening resemblance to the loss of the *Herald of Free Enterprise* off Zeebrugge in 1987, brings into question the safety of roll-on, roll-off ferries with their large bow doors and instability when water penetrates the car decks. (→ 3/10)

Gerry Adams takes hard line during US tour

The Sinn Fein leader got renewed support from Senator Edward Kennedy.

Boston, Tuesday 27
Sinn Fein leader Gerry Adams has been given an enthusiastic welcome in this Irish-American city, home of the Kennedy clan. He is not pulling any punches after controversially being given a visa by President Clinton at Edward Kennedy's urging. In an interview with the *Boston Herald*, he is quoted as warning that IRA violence could return. "None of us can say two or three years up the road that if the causes of the conflict aren't resolved that another IRA leadership won't come along. Because this has always happened." His words are seen in London as vindication of John Major's demand that the IRA must agree to a "permanent" end to violence. (→ 4/10)

Marines watch as pro-Aristide Haitians die

US soldiers arrest a man suspected of having opened fire on unarmed civilians.

Port-au-Prince, Friday 30
The ease with which US troops came into Haiti earlier this month belied the violence to come. Yesterday, a grenade blast near a crowd of anti-junta protestors killed five people. Today, after a celebratory Mass at Notre Dame Cathedral, pro-Aristide demonstrators marched to commemorate the third anniversary of the coup that ousted the president. The marchers deviated from the planned route, passing a bar frequented by members of the Front for Advancement and Progress in Haiti, a violent anti-Aristide group. A gunman fired on the marchers. Three people were killed, one of whom, believed to be pro-military, was beaten to death. (→ 15/10)

October

1994

Su	Mo	Tu	We	Th	Fr	Sa
						1
2	3	4	5	6	7	8
9	10	11	12	13	14	15
16	17	18	19	20	21	22
23	24	25	26	27	28	29
30	31					

Newmarket, 1
A man is arrested for the murder of Alec Scott, one of Britain's top race-horse trainers.

Peleliu, 1
Palau, an island east of the Philippines, becomes independent after 47 years as a US-administered UN trust territory.

London, 1
Buckingham Palace closes its doors to visitors after an eight-week tourist season that netted a profit of £2.8 million.

Hungary, 1
Sales of paprika, one of the country's main exports, are suspended after the discovery of lead-rich red paint in samples of the spice.

London, 2
The Equal Opportunities Commission says that women in Britain earn about three-quarters as much as men.

Turku, Finland, 3
Investigators confirm that the forward cargo door of the *Estonia* broke off after the locks failed.

Washington, 3
Agriculture Secretary Mike Espy, under investigation for accepting gifts from companies that do business with his department, resigns.

London, 3
The High Court grants £504 million in compensation, the largest civil damages award in British legal history, to investors who suffered losses on the Lloyd's insurance market.

St Petersburg, 4
The Hermitage Museum agrees to show more than 70 French Impressionist and Post-Impressionist paintings seized by Soviet troops in Germany at the end of World War II.

Wirral, 5
Britain's oldest man, 109-year-old William Proctor, dies.

Sarajevo, 6
Bosnian fighters admit they killed and mutilated 20 Serb soldiers. (→ 31)

Monza, Italy, 8
Vladislav Bobrik becomes the first Russian to win the Tour of Lombardy bicycle race.

Former cavalry officer claims he had affair with Princess of Wales

Diana with James Hewitt, a major in the Household Cavalry until last March.

London, Monday 3
Major James Hewitt, formerly of the Household Cavalry, claims in a book published today that he conducted a five-year affair with the Princess of Wales. In *Princess in Love*, a book written by freelance journalist Anna Pasternak, the polo-playing Hewitt details trysts at Kensington Palace and at his home in Devon. The book revives speculation about the "Squidgy" tapes, purported to be of Diana talking to her lover, supposedly Hewitt.

Buckingham Palace dismissed the fast-selling book as worthless: "We are not going to waste any more time on this tawdry little book." Hewitt's regiment has made its displeasure known by ordering his name to be "entered at the gate", thereby barring him from the barracks. Friends of the princess quote her as saying: "It is simply not true that we ever had sex. He lives in a fantasy world." (→ 17)

Chairman Mao was a decadent, licentious tyrant, biographer asserts

New York, Sunday 2
Mao Tse Tung, worshipped by millions as the "Great Helmsman" of Communist China, is revealed today in a book by Dr Li Zhisui, his personal physician, as a merciless tyrant with disgusting habits who shared the bed from which he rarely stirred with a succession of young concubines. *The Private Life of Chairman Mao* strips the mask of disinformation from Mao. "He was a man who had no friends," writes Li. "He saw everybody as a subject, a slave. The mistake of those who were purged was to see themselves as equal to him. He wanted everybody to be subservient." That Li survived is something he can barely understand. He admits to being as sycophantic as the rest of Mao's court, but while he was grovelling he was making the notes from which he has written this devastating exposé.

Economic reformer to be Brazil's leader

Rio de Janeiro, Monday 3
Brazilians voted overwhelmingly today to make Finance Minister Fernando Henrique Cardoso their next president. The reforming economist's success stems from his *Plan Real*, introduced to curb Brazil's galloping inflation. Where all previous attempts had failed, Cardoso's plan cut the inflation rate from 50% a month to single figures. The plan involves a new currency, the real, tough limits on money supply and a wage freeze.

He is also threatening harsh austerity measures, but for the moment, Brazilians are content. For the first time, the wage packets of the poor are worth as much at the end of the week as they are at the beginning.

Oct. 3. Phil Collins uses a set resembling an industrial wasteland to sing his hit 'I Don't Care Anymore' at Birmingham's National Exhibition Centre.

Mystery death of 50 sect members in Switzerland

The grisly remains of members of the apocalyptic Order of the Solar Temple at Cheiry, and (right) the cult's guru, Belgian homeopath Luc Jouret, aged 46.

Cheiry, Wednesday 5

Firefighters were alerted to a blaze at a farmhouse near this small Swiss village just after midnight. After having put out the fire, they found a shocking sight in rooms beneath the farm's stables: 18 corpses lying in a circle, feet toward the centre. Most had been shot in the head or neck; others had plastic bags covering their heads. They wore ceremonial robes: red-and-black for the men and white-and-gold for the women. In all, 23 bodies were found. The fire was started by a device which set off containers of petrol and which would have completely destroyed the farm if it had worked as planned. At about 3:00am, a similar device at three ski chalets 100 miles away did work, and 25 people died in the fire. Yesterday, five people died in a fire in Morin Heights, near Montreal. The dead were members of an apoca- lyptic cult called the Order of the Solar Temple. Whether the deaths were a ritualistic mass suicide or murder is unclear. Luc Jouret, the cult's leader and owner of the Swiss chalets and the house in Canada, has not been identified among the dead. Police are now hunting him. (→ 13)

Adams convinces US to lift Sinn Fein ban

Washington, Tuesday 4

Sinn Fein leader Gerry Adams won a propaganda victory here yesterday by manoeuvering the Clinton ad- ministration into lifting the long- standing ban on official contact with Sinn Fein. Complaining that he was not being accorded equal treatment with the representatives of other Northern Ireland parties, Adams threatened to boycott meetings with low-level officials. President Clin- ton, already under pressure from political heavyweights led by Sena- tor Edward Kennedy, caved in and asked Vice-President Al Gore to telephone Adams with the message that the ban had been lifted. The British Embassy said it was "a mat- ter for the Americans". (→ 13)

Labour's leftists inflict an embarrassing setback on Tony Blair

Blackpool, Thursday 6

The Labour Party's left wing turned on Tony Blair at the party's confer- ence here today and reminded their reforming new leader that the so- cialist principles on which the party was founded are still alive. They voted to retain the basic Clause Four, which commits Labour to the public ownership of the means of production, distribution and ex- change. Jim Mearns, who proposed the resolution, set the tone for the vote by quoting from the socialist anthem, "The Red Flag". "Let's not just sing about it," he said. "Let's do it, raise the scarlet standard high and keep the red flag flying here." Blair, pointing out that the vote was 50.9% to 49.1%, shrugged off his embarrassment. He remains deter- mined to review Clause Four.

The new Labour leader remains undaunted despite his defeat on Clause Four.

October

Saddam provokes new crisis in Gulf

Iraq, Monday 10
Saddam Hussein began moving two divisions of the elite Republican Guard toward Kuwait last week, the first brigades arriving just north of the border on Friday. President Clinton immediately began beefing up US forces in the Persian Gulf. Over the weekend, the Iraqis continued the move south, amassing 60,000 troops and 700 tanks within 10 miles of the Kuwaiti border. Today, Iraq made a surprise announcement of a withdrawal, but the Pentagon said they had seen no sign of it. President Clinton continues to build up US forces, sending Saddam an unmistakable message that an invasion of Kuwait would provoke an overwhelming response. (→13)

Glasgow expletives in Booker Prize row

London, Tuesday 11
The Booker Prize lived up to its reputation for controversy when it was awarded to James Kelman, the Glaswegian author, for *How late it was, how late*, a monologue in the Glaswegian vernacular in which he uses the "F word" 21 times in the first three pages. It is the story of an ex-convict who gets drunk and is beaten up and blinded by the police. Julia Neuberger, one of the judges, says the award is a disgrace. Kelman says objections to his language are "another form of imperialism".

Hollywood film war as a studio is born

Los Angeles, Wednesday 12
Comparing their association to the creation in 1919 of United Artists, which brought together Douglas Fairbanks, Mary Pickford and D W Griffith, three of Hollywood's most powerful tycoons said today that they were forming a new studio. It is rumoured that the announcement is a prelude by the partners – director Steven Spielberg, record and movie producer David Geffen and former Disney executive Jeffrey Katzenberg – to making a play for the Japanese-owned studio MCA-Universal.

Russian money crisis as ruble goes under

Moscow, Wednesday 12
President Boris Yeltsin summarily sacked his acting Finance Minister Sergei Dubinin today, accusing him of endangering Russia's economic security as the ruble crashed catastrophically, losing one fifth of its value. There is wild talk of financial saboteurs and a "mystery figure" who has sold off billions of rubles. Yeltsin has ordered the secret service to find out "who is behind" the conspiracy. Meanwhile, Russians look at the soaring prices of imported food and despair.

Major warns Tories

Bournemouth, Friday 14
John Major refused to "lurch to the right" and made a safety-first speech to close the Tory conference today. His message of "steady as she goes" was a blunt rejection of the demand made by Employment Secretary Michael Portillo to put "clear blue water" between the Tories and Labour before the next election. Portillo's speech had brought cheers, and the right-wingers looked disappointed when Major emphasised that his government would be "cautious, pragmatic and safe" in a turbulent world. "Change for the sake of change", he said, "should never appeal to any Conservative."

October 9. Catwalk couture: Bella Freud creations (left) and seductive elegance from Workers for Freedom were hits at the British Fashion Week.

Loyalists announce ceasefire in Northern Ireland

Belfast, Thursday 13

The three main Loyalist terrorist groups in Northern Ireland have announced a ceasefire to match that of the IRA, now seven weeks old. A statement issued by the Combined Loyalist Military Command in northern Belfast this morning said that the "CLMC will universally cease all operational hostilities as from 12 midnight on Thursday the 13th October 1994. The permanence of our ceasefire will be completely dependent upon the continued cessation of all nationalist/republican violence; the sole responsibility for a return to war lies with them." This

move by the Loyalists, who have killed more than 900 people in 25 years of violence, has been greeted with enormous relief. Irish Prime Minister Albert Reynolds said it marked the "closure of a tragic chapter in our history", while John Major, more cautious, said it was "another very important part of the jigsaw falling into place". In another move, the government let it be known it was looking more at the IRA's deeds than its words and was making a "working assumption" the IRA has given up violence for good. That being so, there could be talks with Sinn Fein by Christmas. (→ 21)

A hostage soldier is murdered in Israel

Jerusalem, Friday 14

An Israeli soldier was killed tonight when troops stormed the house where he was being held hostage by Hamas, the radical Islamic organization which was using him to bargain for the release of the group's founder and 200 prisoners. Israeli intelligence agents discovered that Corporal Nachson Waxman, 19, was being held in the village of Bir Nabala on the West Bank and the attack went in an hour before the deadline set by Hamas. The assault team was held up by steel shutters, its commander was killed and Waxman was executed. Three Palestinians died in the shootout.

President Aristide back in Haiti after spending three years in exile

Port-au-Prince, Saturday 15

Thousands of Haitians crowded the streets here today to catch a glimpse of the small man surrounded by a swarm of US-trained bodyguards. President Jean-Bertrand Aristide has finally returned to Haiti after three years in exile. He faces a difficult and short term in power; he leaves office in 16 months and by law cannot be re-elected. Beyond the physical danger from his armed enemies, Aristide faces the task of rebuilding a country devastated by international sanctions and three years of misrule. Haiti will have financial help from the US, but the people's expectations may exceed what can be achieved in the Western hemisphere's poorest nation. (→ 18)

Nobels for peacemakers, Japanese author

Kenzaburo Oe, 59, Literature Nobel.

Oslo, Friday 14

The Nobel Peace Prize has been won jointly by Yitzhak Rabin and Shimon Peres of Israel and Yasser Arafat of the PLO for replacing "war and hate" with "peace and cooperation", but the award is surrounded by controversy. Kare Kristiansen, a member of the selection committee, has resigned in protest, explaining that Arafat's past "is too tainted with violence".

The Literature Prize has gone to Kenzaburo Oe, a Japanese writer haunted by his nation's humiliation in World War II. The committee said his work "forms a disconcerting picture of the human predicament".

October 14. Ffyona Campbell reaches John o' Groats and becomes the first woman to walk around the world. She walked 20 to 30 miles a day for 11 years and wore out 100 pairs of shoes to complete the 19,586-mile journey.

October

Prince of Wales tells of his agony over failed marriage to Diana

Prince Charles felt driven to wed Diana by his father, the Duke of Edinburgh.

London, Monday 17
Britain is enthralled by the revelations about the Prince of Wales and Diana contained in his biography by Jonathan Dimbleby. In the book, which he has seen and authorised, the prince speaks of the "total agony of the situation". The collapse of his loveless marriage, he told friends, "has all the ingredients of a Greek tragedy. ... I never thought it would end up like this. How could I ever have got it so wrong?" The book suggests that he was forced into the marriage by his father, who argued that by entertaining Lady Di at Balmoral he was compromising her. Today, Prince Philip delivered a back-handed rebuke to his son: "I've never made any comment about any member of the family in 40 years, and I'm not going to start now."

Chancellor Kohl wins crucial German vote

Bonn, Sunday 16
Helmut Kohl claimed victory in Germany's general election today but his majority of over 100 has been slashed to 10. Kohl dismissed suggestions that this majority would be unworkable and that he should ally his Christian Democratic Union with the Social Democrats. "We have a working majority," he said, "and we will continue with the present coalition." Also worrying for him is the success of the reformed East German Communists – a message of voter discontent.

Reporter in Moscow killed by bomb blast

Moscow, Monday 17
Investigative reporter Dmitri Kholodov was killed today when a briefcase, supposedly containing documents revealing corruption in the army, exploded as he opened it. The newsroom of the liberal *Moskovski Komsomolets* was wrecked, and he died on the way to hospital. Kholodov was probing the former Western Group of Forces, based in Germany, whose commander, General Matvei Burlakov, has been accused of turning his forces into "a structuralised criminal system".

US and North Korea to sign nuclear deal

Washington, Tuesday 18
"North Korea has agreed to freeze its existing nuclear programme and to accept international inspection of all existing facilities. This agreement represents the first step on the road to a nuclear-free peninsula." With these words, President Clinton announced his approval of a long-sought treaty. In return, the country will get new nuclear-energy reactors, paid for mostly by South Korea and Japan, that produce less waste plutonium which can be used to make nuclear bombs.

Oct. 16. Michael Schumacher's return to the Formula One circuit after his two-race suspension cost Damon Hill first place in the Spanish Grand Prix.

Oct. 19. Sinead O'Connor models a John Rocha gown in Paris.

Queen Elizabeth II makes historic visit to Russia

A glittering welcome for the Queen and President Boris Yeltsin at the Bolshoi.

St Petersburg, Thursday 20
The Queen ended her mission to Russia today by touring a palace which once belonged to her Russian relatives and visiting the cathedral where the murdered Tsar Nicholas is to be buried. It has been an excellent visit despite an element of Russian chaos. The Queen has not met as many ordinary Russians as she would have liked, but neither has she been embraced in Boris Yeltsin's bear-like hug. At a state banquet in the Kremlin, she told him: "You and I have spent most of our lives believing that this evening could never happen. I hope you are as delighted as I am to be proved wrong. I am the first British sovereign to visit Moscow. You are the first president of an independent Russia."

A sunny walkabout on Red Square.

Muslim suicide bomber kills 21 people in Tel Aviv bus carnage

Tel Aviv, Wednesday 19
A suicide bomber blew up a bus in the centre of Tel Aviv today, killing 21 people and wounding 45 in the bloodiest terrorist attack in Israel for 16 years. The fanatical Islamic movement Hamas said it was one of their "martyrs" who blew himself and the bus to pieces and threatened to carry out more suicide attacks on Jewish targets. The Israelis have reacted by imposing harsh security measures, sealing off Arab areas from the Jewish heartland. Prime Minister Yitzhak Rabin, who cut short his visit to Britain to return, blamed Iran for the bombing. (→ 27)

Race, IQ and class debate raging in US

United States, Wednesday 19
The United States is currently embroiled in a controversy over the relationship of intelligence to race and class. The debate, which has often raged in the US, is rekindled by three new books: *Race, Evolution and Behavior: A Life History Perspective* by J. Phillipe Rushton, *The Decline of Intelligence in America: A Strategy for National Renewal* by Seymour W. Itzkoff and *The Bell Curve: Intelligence and Class Structure in American Life* by Charles Murray and the late Richard Herrnstein. All three books assert that IQ is a real and accurate indicator of intelligence and that it is correlated to job success and rates of crime and other social pathologies. The authors say that a low-IQ underclass is reproducing more quickly than the "cognitive elite", lowering the intelligence of the country. They also point out that blacks make up a large proportion of this underclass and that blacks as a group score lower on IQ tests than whites.

While some people say the books spell out a hard truth that the country must face, others discount them as unscientific and racist. Many scientists reject the value of IQ tests, and there is little if any agreement on how much of a person's intelligence is inherited.

Hollywood's tough guy Burt Lancaster is felled by a heart attack

Los Angeles, Thursday 20
Burt Lancaster, the veteran Hollywood actor who was at his best playing the humane tough guy, died of a heart attack at his home here tonight. Born in a rough Irish area of New York on November 2, 1913, he won a scholarship to New York University but dropped out to become a trapeze artist. He made his first film, *The Killers*, in 1946 and went on to appear in more than 70 including *The Birdman of Alcatraz*, *The Swimmer*, *Local Hero*, *The Leopard* and *Tough Guys*. Four times nominated, he won only one Oscar, for his role as Elmer Gantry.

October

Sri Lanka peace talks halted after bomb kills opposition leader

Presidential candidate Gamini Dissanayake and 50 others died in the blast.

Colombo, Monday 24
The Sri Lankan government called off its peace talks with the Tamil rebels and clamped a state of emergency on this troubled island today following the murder by a suicide bomber of Gamini Dissanayake, the opposition candidate in the presidential elections. Fifty-six others, including opposition leaders, died when the bomber, believed to be a woman, exploded the device. Dissanayake, 53, was on the Tamil hit-list because, as a minister in a previous government, he had been responsible for bringing Indian troops into Sri Lanka to fight the rebels – a move which cost Indian Premier Rajiv Gandhi his life at the hands of a similar suicide bomber. (→10/11)

Minister resigns as 'sleaze' row rocks MPs

London, Tuesday 25
The prime minister announced a far-reaching inquiry into allegations of "sleaze" in public life last night as Westminster indulged in a frenzy of rumour following the forced resignation of Corporate Affairs Minister Neil Hamilton. Hamilton, whose denial of taking money from Mohamed al-Fayed, the chairman of Harrods, to table parliamentary questions had been accepted by Major, was forced out of office by what the prime minister called other "unconnected allegations". Hamilton is furious. In a letter to Major, he said it was "sad and deeply disturbing" that he had been forced from office because of a "foully motivated rumour and media witch-hunt". He said he had not been paid by Fayed: "Nor have I acted in return for favours." The affair boils on, and other ministers are being named. Major announced that he has reported Fayed to the Director of Public Prosecutions for what is described as "attempted blackmail".

Hong Kong's team break rugby record

Kuala Lumpur, Thursday 27
The scoreboard looked as if it were tallying the runs in a cricket match rather than an international rugby game here when Hong Kong broke the world record by defeating Singapore 164-13. Playing in the Asian qualifying tournament to enter next year's World Cup, Singapore were thoroughly trounced 90-3 by South Korea and then 69-5 by Thailand before today's humiliation.

Major Arctic oil spill threatens environmental nightmare in Russia

Western experts say some 270,000 tons of oil have spewed from the pipeline.

Moscow, Wednesday 26
Thousands of tons of crude oil are spilling out of a leaking pipeline near Usinsk, 60 miles south of the Arctic Circle. News of the spill came not from Moscow but from Washington, where officials insist that the Arctic's ecology is so fragile that any spill is an "international issue". They have offered help in cleaning up the damage and preventing pollution of the Pechora River. A local preservation group said that 23 holes appeared in the pipeline in August but that oil was pumped through it for another three weeks, the spilt oil being contained by an earthen dyke. The disaster occurred when the dyke was washed away by heavy rain three weeks ago and the oil gushed out, contaminating large areas of virgin land.

Clinton fails to win peace pledge from Syria

An extremely tough and wily negotiator, Syria's President Hafez Assad (right).

Jerusalem, Thursday 27
Bill Clinton, who yesterday witnessed the signing of a peace treaty ending 46 years of hostilities between Jordan and Israel, flew to Damascus today to meet President Hafez Assad. He flew back here tonight after his six-hour visit, the first to Syria by a US president in 20 years, and gave a joint press conference with Israeli Premier Yitzhak Rabin. No great advances were made in the president's meeting with Assad, but he said his talks led him to believe that Syria's leaders "understand that it is time to make peace. There will still be a good deal of hard bargaining before a breakthrough, but they are serious about proceeding." (→ 10/11)

Santer rebuffs Brittan over EU Commission

Say cheese, please: the 21 members of the incoming European Commission.

Luxembourg, Saturday 29
Sir Leon Brittan has emerged as the big loser after a day of fierce bargaining at the Chateau de Senningen over the allocation of jobs in the EU. The president-elect, Jacques Santer, has stripped Sir Leon, the UK's senior commissioner, of his responsibility for relations with the former Soviet Union and the new East European democracies, and these crucial areas have been given to his rival, Hans van den Broek, the Dutch commissioner. Sir Leon is threatening to resign, but John Major has urged him to stay and represent Britain's interests. Former Labour leader Neil Kinnock, newly appointed UK commissioner, was given the transport portfolio.

Hubble telescope rejuvenates the universe

Greenbelt, Maryland, Wednesday 26
Astronomers working on the Hubble Space Telescope project to study the scale and age of the universe announced their first findings today. According to the data sent back from the telescope, the universe may be much younger than scientists previously thought – between 8 billion and 12 billion years old. Earlier calculations put the oldest stars at 15 to 18 billion years old.

Bosnian fighters launch successful offensive

Sarajevo, Monday 31
The Bosnian government's 5th Army Corps has staged a spectacular breakout in northwestern Bosnia, forcing the Serbs to flee in some disarray from 100 square miles of territory to the east and south of the government-held town of Bihac. According to UN spokesman Lt-Col Tim Spicer, "The Bosnian Serb army crumbled. Their command and control system is gone." (→ 4/11)

Oct. 29. Francisco Duran, aged 26, fires an SKS assault rifle at the White House before being overpowered by two young bystanders and arrested.

October 31. The Duke of Edinburgh becomes the first member of the royal family to visit Israel since the Jewish state was created in May 1948.

Su	Mo	Tu	We	Th	Fr	Sa
		1	2	3	4	5
6	7	8	9	10	11	12
13	14	15	16	17	18	19
20	21	22	23	24	25	26
27	28	29	30			

Casablanca, 1
The Middle East-North Africa Economic Summit ends; Israel and Arab countries agree to cooperate on tourism and commerce.

Algeria, 1
Five Muslim Scouts are killed in a bomb attack during commemorations of the 40th anniversary of the beginning of the war for independence from France.

Washington, 1
The government announces it will increase aid to Ulster from $20 million to $30 million a year. (→ 3)

Barcelona, 2
Manchester United are defeated 4-0 by Barcelona in a Champions League Group A match.

London, 2
Sir John Gielgud announces his retirement from the stage.

London, 3
Roland "Tiny" Rowland is forced to resign as chief executive and joint managing director of Lonrho plc.

London, 3
The Royal Navy announces plans to eliminate the traditional bell-bottom sailors' trousers after 137 years.

Hong Kong, 3
China and Britain agree on the financing for the colony's £12.5 billion airport.

United States, 4
Science magazine details the first discovery of a fossilised embryo of a meat-eating dinosaur.

Union, South Carolina, 4
Susan Smith is charged with murder after confessing that she sank her car with her two children inside in a lake; she had previously claimed that they had been kidnapped in a carjacking.

Ulster, 5
Mivan Marine say they are designing a £100 million exact replica of the *Titanic* for use by a Japanese company as a floating hotel.

DEATH

5. Sir Patrick Dean, British diplomat (*16/3/09).

Three Western hostages murdered by Khmer Rouge in Cambodia

The captives in August: Jean-Michel Braquet, David Wilson and Mark Slater.

Phnom Penh, Wednesday 2
The bodies of three Western hostages murdered by the Khmer Rouge have been recovered from their jungle graves and were brought here today. The three young men, Mark Slater, 28, from Northamptonshire, David Wilson, 29, from Australia, and Frenchman Jean-Michel Braquet, 27, had been abducted from a train on July 26 and held in the guerrilla stronghold on Vine Mountain, 90 miles south of the capital. On September 28, while government forces pounded the mountain with heavy guns, they were bound, blindfolded and led into the jungle to be shot. In London, the government condemned the killings as barbaric.

UK's last hangman, Syd Dernley, is dead

Mansfield, Tuesday 1
Sydney Dernley, 73, apprentice hangman to Albert Pierrepoint and Britain's last surviving executioner, died in his bed at home here today. He took part in the execution of 28 men, including that of Timothy Evans, who was posthumously pardoned. Dernley, a colliery welder, had a macabre sense of humour and boasted that he and Pierrepoint had carried out the fastest hanging on record: that of James Inglis, in just seven seconds. He was paid three guineas for each hanging.

Dwingeloo 1, a new galaxy, is discovered

Britain, Wednesday 2
Astronomers at a Dutch observatory have discovered a new galaxy about 10 million light years away from Earth. Dwingeloo 1, named after the radio telescope that found it, is a spiral galaxy estimated to have about one third of the mass of the Milky Way. In the report detailing their findings in this week's *Nature*, the British, Dutch and American team say that Dwingeloo 1, located behind the constellation Cassiopeia, may in fact be only the central portion of a much larger galaxy.

Heseltine is forced to abandon PO plan

London, Thursday 3
Michael Heseltine, President of the Board of Trade, has been forced to abandon his plans for privatising the Post Office following the refusal of a dozen Tory rebels to agree to any of the options he suggested. This defeat is being seen not only as a humiliation for Heseltine but also the end of the Thatcherite revolution of the right. It also underlines John Major's perilous position where a handful of rebels can hold his government to ransom and force the withdrawal of major legislation.

Flash flood and fuel explosion devastate a Nile Valley community

Durunka, Egypt, Thursday 3
This farming town about 200 miles southeast of Cairo has been devastated by a catastrophe of biblical proportions. Torrential rains, the worst in Egypt in 50 years, began Tuesday, and early yesterday a fuel depot here exploded, releasing burning fuel to be spread by the flood waters. The floods have carried off trucks and cars, demolished homes and flushed out coffins from cemetery crypts. This morning, provincial authorities put the death toll at 372, but civil defence workers continue to find victims who have either been drowned or have been burned to death. At least 500 people have been found dead so far.

At least 500 have died with the death toll still rising in the town of Durunka.

Bosnia Serbs strike back

The Serb counterattack around Bihac comes after Bosnian Muslim advances.

Sarajevo, Friday 4

The Bosnian Serbs have begun their retaliation for the surprising defeats, which culminated in the fall of the strategic town of Kupres last night, that they have suffered at the hands of the Croats and Muslims in the past two weeks. They opened their attack on the UN safe area of Bihac today, bombarding the city with rockets. The UN accused the Serbs of "terrorism" and NATO war-planes screamed overhead, looking for the rocket positions, but the UN took the political decision not to launch an airstrike, fearing that any further humiliation of the Serbs might be counterproductive to the peace process. There is little indication, however, that the Serbs are thinking of peace. Today, Radovan Karadzic, their leader, announced a complete mobilisation and called for all-out war. (→ 11)

Dublin seeks to calm fears of Protestants

Dublin, Thursday 3

Irish Premier Albert Reynolds promised today there would be no change in the political status of Ulster without the consent of the majority of its people. His government, he said, was prepared to approve a radical change in the Irish constitution, which claims sovereignty over the north and is a major obstacle to the peace process. Seeking to calm northern fears of being gobbled up by the south, he said: "We are aware of the fears of the Unionist community, so we are prepared to insert the principle of consent in the Irish constitution." (→ 17)

French press reveals Mitterrand's 'secret'

France, Thursday 3

Paris Match today broke a long-standing French taboo on reporting on the private lives of public figures; the cover features a picture of President Mitterrand with his 20-year-old daughter by his mistress. The to-do here is not over the well established fact of the president's "second family" nor about him taking his *fille naturelle* with him on official overseas trips and inviting her to state dinners. The political and publishing milieu is worried that the French press may be becoming too "Anglo-Saxon", that is, too willing to create scandals to sell their publications.

Nov. 5. Pedal power: Tony Rominger of Switzerland breaks his own world cycling record by covering an amazing 55.291 kilometres in one hour.

Nov. 5. Former President Ronald Reagan, 83, reveals that he is suffering from the early stages of Alzheimer's disease, an incurable brain disorder.

Nov. 5. By George! George Foreman, 45, beats Michael Moorer, 27, to regain the world heavyweight title he lost to Muhammad Ali 20 years ago.

November

1994

Su	Mo	Tu	We	Th	Fr	Sa
		1	2	3	4	5
6	7	8	9	10	11	12
13	14	15	16	17	18	19
20	21	22	23	24	25	26
27	28	29	30			

Suzuka, 6
Damon Hill wins the Japanese Grand Prix.

New York, 6
Mexican German Silva wins the New York Marathon with a time of 2:11:21.

Washington, 6
President Clinton announces the withdrawal of troops from Haiti by December 1 and from Kuwait by the end of the year.

Britain, 6
A survey of Britain's top 212 companies shows that 84% of the directors think a single European currency would be good for British businesses; 8% believe it would be damaging.

London, 7
The government approves the development of a major new oilfield in the Atlantic west of the Shetlands which could eventually produce about one third of Britain's oil output.

Hebron, 7
Israel reopens the Tomb of the Patriarchs, closed since the massacre eight months ago.

Britain, 8
A *Times* survey shows four out of five women studying at Oxford have been victims of some sort of sexual harassment.

London, 9
Goalkeeper Bruce Grobbelaar, now playing for Southampton, denies accusations that he took bribes to throw matches when he was playing for Liverpool.

Baghdad, 10
Iraq recognises Kuwait's sovereignty.

Huambo, 10
Angolan government forces overrun UNITA headquarters; the rebels say they will not sign a planned peace treaty. (→ 20)

Gaza, 11
A suicide bomber kills three Israeli soldiers and wounds at least 12 Israelis and Palestinians. (→ 18)

London, 12
England beat Romania 54-3 in the first of the rugby season's internationals.

DEATH

10. Carmen McRae, American jazz singer (*8/4/22).

Democrats humiliated by poll verdict

Clinton tries to put a brave face on the results, while Newt Gingrich promises to make life tough for the US president.

Washington, Wednesday 9
Republicans won control of both houses of Congress for the first time in 40 years in yesterday's elections. In the Senate, 53 of the 100 seats are now Republican, and in the House there are now 230 Republicans and 204 Democrats. Voters turned out Democratic governors as well, including New York's Mario Cuomo, defeated by George Pataki; a majority of the statehouses are now Republican. Republicans say the results are a rebuke by voters to Bill Clinton, who said today, "They sent us a clear message – I got it."

Cooperation between the White House and the new majority will be difficult. Although Bob Dole, the Senate's Republican leader, seems willing to make deals with the president, Jesse Helms, who is likely to head the powerful Senate Foreign Relations Committee, and Newt Gingrich, expected to be the next House Speaker, are more combative. Both these right-wing Southerners have built reputations as "bomb throwers" and have blasted Bill Clinton at every opportunity. (→ 22)

Nov. 7. Torrential rains in Lombardy, Liguria and Piedmont, along with the worst storms in northern Italy in 80 years, have left 59 people dead, thousands of others homeless and caused damage estimated at nearly £4,000 million.

Israel-Jordan peace treaty signed in Galilee

It was the Jordanian monarch's first public appearance on Israeli territory.

Sri Lankan widow wins general elections

Chandrika Bandaranaike Kumaratunga's husband and father were murdered.

Israel, Thursday 10

King Hussein of Jordan made his first official visit to Israel today to sign and exchange ratified copies of the peace treaty which he and Israeli Prime Minister Yitzhak Rabin had first signed on October 26.

The signing ceremony was held on the lawn of Gabrial House, a marble mansion built on the shore of the Sea of Galilee by an Israeli to accommodate Arab-Israeli peace-making efforts. The prime minister praised the king and called the peace treaty a "most beautiful act". King Hussein replied: "This is an honourable peace, a balanced peace, a peace that will last because from the first instance it was our determination to make it so."

Colombo, Thursday 10

Sri Lankan Premier Chandrika Kumaratunga swept to victory by almost two million votes in the presidential elections today. Campaigning under the sign of the dove, her party, the People's Alliance, won in all 22 districts, crushing the United National Party, which had ruled for 17 troubled years until last August's parliamentary election. A macabre aspect of the election and a judgement on Sri Lankan politics is that Kumaratunga's father, a former prime minister, and her husband, a popular film star and politician, were both assassinated. Her election opponent, Srima Dissanayake, ran only after the murder of her husband three weeks ago.

Europeans outraged by US Bosnia move

London, Friday 11

A serious rift opened between Washington and its outraged European allies last night following President Clinton's decision to order US warships in the Adriatic to halt the enforcement of the arms embargo on the Bosnian Muslims. The Pentagon emphasised that the US would not supply arms to the Muslims but that it would no longer block shipments from other countries and would no longer pass intelligence reports on such shipments to its NATO allies. A White House official explained it was the only means the administration had of blunting Congressional demands for the US to take the more serious step of actually supplying arms to the Muslims. While recognising that the US move will have little effect on the supply of arms, the Europeans are dismayed at the signals it is sending to the warring factions in Bosnia. (→ 20)

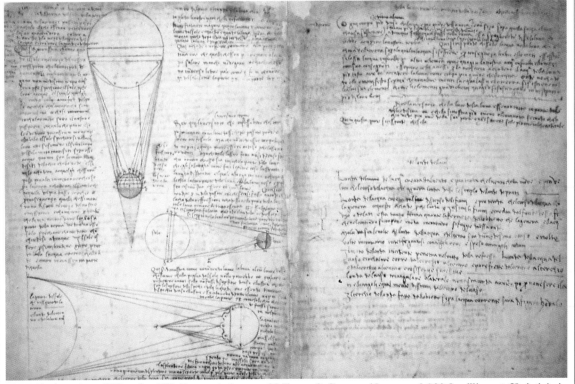

Nov. 12. American billionaire Bill Gates, chairman of Microsoft Corp, paid a record $30.8 million at Christie's in New York for this 72-page scientific treatise written and illustrated by Leonardo da Vinci between 1506 and 1510.

November

Massachusetts, 13
A 79-year-old golfer drops dead after shooting his first ever hole-in-one.

Sweden, 13
Voters approve membership of the European Union.

Puerto Rico, 13
Americans Fred Couples and Davis Love win the Golf World Cup for the third straight time.

Jakarta, 15
The 18 member nations of the Asia-Pacific Economic Cooperation forum agree to create the world's largest free trade area by the year 2020.

Buenos Aires, 15
Prince Andrew begins a four-day visit to Argentina.

Jerusalem, 15
President Thomas Klestil of Austria apologises for his country's role during World War II.

Montevideo, 16
The former mayor of Nice, Jacques Médecin, is extradited to face corruption charges in France.

Kiev, 16
The Ukrainian parliament ratifies the Nuclear Nonproliferation Treaty.

Seoul, 16
South Korea orders all its diplomats to leave Algeria.

Tokyo, 17
Sony Corporation announces that the Hollywood studios it bought in 1989, Tristar and Columbia, have suffered losses of $3.2 billion.

Cape Town, 17
President Mandela signs a law allowing blacks to claim land seized under apartheid.

Chartres, France, 18
John Major and President Mitterrand agree to create a Franco-British air force group.

DEATHS

15. Humphrey Berkeley, former Tory MP (*21/2/26).

16. Doris Speed, British television actress (*3/2/1899).

18. Cab Calloway, US bandleader (*25/12/07).

19. Michael Somes, British ballet dancer (*28/9/17).

Nigel Mansell wins the race, Schumacher takes the world title

Adelaide, Sunday 13
Nigel Mansell has won the Australian Grand Prix for the first time; the victory was his 31st on the Formula One circuit.

But the drama in today's race centred on the close competition between Damon Hill and Michael Schumacher for the Formula One drivers' title; the driver who finished first would take the championship. Schumacher was leading on lap 36 when steering problems with his Benetton Ford became apparent. He swerved off to the right but managed to get back on track. When Hill challenged him on the inside, the cars collided. Both were out of the race, and the championship went to Schumacher by one point.

Prime minister challenges Tory Euro-rebels

Westminster, Wednesday 16
Queen Elizabeth II conducted the state opening of Parliament today with the threat of an early general election lending spice to the pomp and ceremony.

Prime Minister John Major has put his future on the line over the controversial Bill to increase Britain's payments to the European Union. He told the Commons he regarded the legislation "inescapably as a matter of confidence" leaving him no option but to call an election if the Tory Euro-rebels combine with the opposition to defeat it. "There is no room for compromise," he stressed. (→ 28)

November 14. Better late than never: A Eurostar high-speed train leaves Waterloo for Paris to inaugurate the Channel Tunnel Passenger service.

Martina plays her final tennis match

New York, Tuesday 15
Martina Navratilova said goodbye in style tonight to a brilliant career which shone for more than 20 years and brought her 167 singles titles. A crowd of 17,000 in Madison Square Garden rose to her as she was played in with Tina Turner's "Simply the Best" and was presented with a gleaming Harley-Davidson. Even losing 6-4, 6-2 to Gabriela Sabatini in the first round of the Virginia Slims championship did not seem to matter. Her adoring fans cheered her as she bounced into the arena carrying a box of tissues. Martina, 38, told them: "Emotionally this has been the most difficult moment because this is the last time. There is no next week. Physically I could still play, but my heart is tired."

Dublin government falls

Albert Reynolds struggled for five days to save his two-year-old coalition.

Thirteen are killed as clashes erupt in Gaza

The street battle broke out when Islamic militants attacked Palestinian police.

Dublin, Thursday 17
Ireland was plunged into political turmoil today when Prime Minister Albert Reynolds resigned "for the good of the nation". He had struggled for five days to save his government following the withdrawal of the Labour Party from the ruling coalition in protest against the appointment of Harry Whelehan, former attorney general, as president of the High Court. Dick Spring, leader of the Labour Party, had objected to Whelehan's delay in extraditing a paedophile Roman Catholic priest to Northern Ireland. The workings of Dublin politics have a touch of farce about them, but this affair has a serious aspect. Reynolds' departure could harm the Irish peace process. (→9/12)

Massive Euro-waste revealed by auditors

Brussels, Wednesday 16
Britain's Euro-rebels have been handed a powerful weapon by the European Court of Auditors, which reported yesterday that fraud and waste cost the EU between £600 million and £4 billion last year. Scams riddle the EU and involve everything from non-existent vineyards to misdirected sugar and milk powder. The report complains of weak controls and inadequate documentation throughout the Union.

Gaza, Friday 18
Yasser Arafat's police killed at least 12 people and wounded as many as 200 in street battles here today with Palestinian protestors. The Palestinian police say that Islamic extremists fired first and that one policeman was killed and 10 wounded.

Protestors denounced Arafat as a "traitor" for "collaborating" with the former occupiers of the Palestinian territories, and the most extreme of the Islamic hardliners are threatening a civil war. To show their disdain for the new Palestinian authority, many militants detained by the police now respond to their questions in Hebrew.

Mozambique's vote is won by Chissano

Maputo, Saturday 19
The former rebel leader Afonso Dhlakama conceded defeat today as results came in from Mozambique's first multiparty poll, despite his contention that the elections "were not fair". President Joaquim Chissano and his party held on to power: He won 53.3% of the presidential vote, and Frelimo took 129 of the parliamentary seats. Dhlakama's Mozambican National Resistance Movement won 112 seats.

And the winner is ... millions chase National Lottery's first jackpot

Nov. 18. Margaret Thatcher's official coat of arms is unveiled.

London, Saturday 19
The winning numbers in Britain's first National Lottery came up in a TV extravaganza tonight as gambling fever seized the nation; but, much to the organizers' chagrin, no single ticket-holder claimed the jackpot. Instead, the £15.8 million prize was shared by seven punters who selected the winning line. There was some consolation in the fact that many more people than expected won the guaranteed lowest prize of £10 for selecting three correct numbers. But that was not what the gamblers wanted. They wanted the big prize. Camelot, the organizers, estimate that about 25 million people had bought a ticket by the time sales stopped at 7:30pm with £45 million in the kitty. (→11/12)

November

1994

Su	Mo	Tu	We	Th	Fr	Sa
		1	2	3	4	5
6	7	8	9	10	11	12
13	14	15	16	17	18	19
20	21	22	23	24	25	26
27	28	29	30			

Washington, 20
The US denies French claims that it is supplying arms to Bosnian Muslims. (→ 23)

Rio de Janeiro, 20
Hundreds of troops are deployed in the city's slums in an attempt to stem the drug trade.

Britain, 21
Red Rum, the only horse to win the Grand National three times, retires from public life at the age of 29.

Texas, 21
Smoking is banned for inmates and employees in all the state's prisons.

London, 22
The £20,000 Turner Prize is awarded to sculptor Antony Gormley.

New York, 22
The BBC wins five International Emmy Awards.

London, 22
A collector pays a record £25,300 for a 1933 penny.

Chester, 23
Colin McRae becomes the first British driver to win the RAC Rally since 1976.

Nagpur, India, 23
128 people are killed in a stampede when police move in to break up a demonstration.

London, 23
Labradors, Alsatians and golden retrievers are the three most popular dogs in Britain, according to the Kennel Club.

London, 25
Buckingham Palace announces that it will publish annual accounts to show how taxpayers' money is spent.

Cardiff, 26
South Africa's touring rugby union side beat Wales 20-12.

DEATHS

22. Captain Charles Upham, New Zealand army officer, one of only three men to win the Victoria Cross twice (*21/9/08).

23. Erick Hawkins, US ballet dancer (*23/4/09).

24. George Nigel Douglas-Hamilton, Earl of Selkirk, former First Lord of the Admiralty (*4/1/06).

Precarious peace pact signed to end Angola's 19-year civil war

Lusaka, Zambia, Sunday 20
The government of Angola and UNITA rebels signed a peace treaty here today, but there are serious doubts that the war will really come to an end. Fighting continued yesterday, and UNITA leader Jonas Savimbi was not present for the signing. The rebels said he was unable to leave the country because all the airports in the areas they controlled were being bombarded by government forces. In the absence of Savimbi, President Jose Eduardo dos Santos, who was here for the ceremony, designated his foreign minister, Venancio de Moura, to sign the treaty with UNITA's General Eugenio Manuvakola.

Republican firebrand apologises for threat

Washington, Tuesday 22
Jesse Helms, the senator from South Carolina expected to be the next chairman of the Foreign Relations Committee, has embarrassed leaders of his party with his virulent attacks on Bill Clinton. On Friday, he said that Clinton was not fit to be commander-in-chief of the armed forces, and in a newspaper interview published today he warned that if the president visited army bases in his state, he had "better have a bodyguard". After being criticised for the remark, he said he had made a mistake but did not apologise.

Top Tory quits after attack on Europeans

London, Wednesday 23
Tory MP Patrick Nicholls resigned from his post as a vice-chairman of the party tonight after making a scathing attack on Britain's EU partners. In an article in the *Western Morning News*, he wrote that France "has the nerve to represent itself as a nation of resistance fighters ... when, in fact, it was a nation of collaborators" and that Germany's unique contribution "has been to plunge Europe into two world wars". As for the "lesser countries", they "insult us to the tune of their banging begging bowls".

138 nations agree to fight criminal groups

Naples, Wednesday 23
At an international conference, 138 nations pledged to work together to fight against worldwide organized crime. The main concern here was money laundering, which has grown more complex with the collapse of communism's control of banks and borders in Eastern Europe. It is estimated that organized criminal groups handle some $750 billion in dirty money every year. Drugs remain the big money-maker for international mobsters, but they also smuggle human organs for transplants and nuclear materials.

Nov. 22. Kenneth Branagh is made an officer of the French Order of Arts and Letters.

Nov. 23. Going strong since April 1, 1960, Dr Martens, whose footwear has a worldwide cult following, opens an emporium in London's Covent Garden.

Alliance in crisis as Serbs defy NATO air strikes

Sarajevo, Wednesday 23

NATO fighters struck at Bosnian Serb SAM-2 missile sites at Otoka today, 15 miles north-east of the Bihac pocket. Twenty fighters attacked the missile sites which had attempted to shoot down two patrolling Royal Navy Sea Harriers yesterday. Two other SAM sites locked onto the raiding planes on their way to the target, and these too were attacked "in self-defence". Today's raids follow Monday's strike on a Serb airfield in Ubdina, Croatia, in which some 50 aircraft were involved, making it the biggest bomb raid in NATO's 45-year history. It has emerged, however, that NATO pulled its punches on the Udbina raid, taking out SAM missiles and cratering the runway but not touching the Serb warplanes parked on the perimeter of the airfield for fear of causing "collateral damage". The raids have brought nothing but defiance from the Serbs, who are pressing on with their assault on Bihac. Instead they have emphasised the dissension which is threatening the NATO alliance. While the Americans are demanding more forceful military action, the European powers insist they are in Bosnia for humanitarian purposes only and are talking of pulling out altogether. It appears that Britain and France agreed to the attack on Udbina only because the Serbs were using it to raid Bihac, where 1,200 Bangladeshi UN troops are cut off. (→ 30)

A Serb SAM-2 missile near Bihac: The ageing Soviet-built weapon, called 'Guideline' by NATO, still packs a big punch.

Crucial intelligence revealed by hacker

Britain, Thursday 24

The Independent revealed today how a computer hacker managed to gain access to telephone numbers and addresses for MI6, MI5, secret Ministry of Defence installations and other sensitive material. The hacker, while employed at British Telecom as a temporary worker, obtained computer passwords which allowed him to access the state secrets.

Berlusconi is fighting for political survival

Naples, Wednesday 23

Italian Premier Silvio Berlusconi has been placed under investigation in connection with bribes allegedly paid by his company, Fininvest, to tax inspectors. "I have never corrupted anyone," he said. "I have nothing to fear." He announced today that he would sell his majority stake in his media empire on the stock market. (→ 6/12)

Quarantine for pets debate rages in UK

London, Wednesday 23

A report today by the Commons Select Committee on Agriculture arguing that quarantine is no longer the most effective way of keeping rabies at bay raised the usual hackles. The RSPCA gave the report "a cautious welcome", but the Royal College of Veterinary Surgeons opposed dropping quarantine until "an effective alternative is found".

November 23. Arnold Schwarzenegger changes from terminator to incubator in his new US release, *Junior*, a comedy co-starring Emma Thompson.

Nov. 26. Giuseppe Verdi's opera *Aida*, with Wilhelmina Fernandez in the title role, is performed outside an ancient Egyptian temple near Luxor.

November

1994

Su	Mo	Tu	We	Th	Fr	Sa
		1	2	3	4	5
6	7	8	9	10	11	12
13	14	15	16	17	18	19
20	21	22	23	24	25	26
27	28	29	30			

London, 28
The Equal Opportunities Commission reports that at least four million women are on low pay.

Brussels, 28
The EU lifts its eight-year-old arms embargo on Syria.

Uruguay, 28
Julio Sanguinetti wins the presidential election.

Berlin, 28
Lamerica, by Italian director Gianni Amello, wins the European Film Academy's award for best picture.

London, 28
Britain protests to Madrid against the partial closure of the border between Spain and Gibraltar.

London, 29
Ronald "Buster" Edwards, 62, who served nine years for his part in the 1963 Great Train Robbery, commits suicide.

Budapest, 29
Hungary drops plans to host the 1996 Expo world fair.

Katmandu, 29
King Birendra names Man Mohan Adhikary as Nepal's first Communist premier.

Westminster, 29
Chancellor Kenneth Clarke unveils a cautious budget aimed at keeping "the recovery on track".

London, 30
The Fiat Punto is named Car of the Year 1995 by a panel of 56 motoring journalists from 21 countries; Volkswagen's new Polo is runner-up.

Hong Kong, 30
Prior to moving to Singapore, Jardine Matheson, the oldest trading house in the colony, bids farewell to the bourse.

Paris, 30
A government committee recommends that the consumption of soft drugs be allowed in private.

DEATHS

28. Jerry Rubin, 1960s US radical (*14/7/38).

29. Grand Ayatollah Mohammed Ali Araki, spiritual leader of the world's 100 million Shiite Muslims (*1884).

Norwegian voters say no to Europe

Anne Enger Lahnstein, head of the anti-European Union Centre Party, addresses a crowd of her supporters in Oslo.

Norway, Monday 28
Norwegians have again said no to the European Union. In a referendum which elicited a record turnout of 88.5%, the "nei" won with a clear majority of 52.2%, only slightly smaller than the one in 1972 which rejected joining the European Economic Community, as it was called then. The two largest cities, Oslo and Bergen, were the centres of the pro-Europeans, who argued that going it alone would cut them off from lucrative trade. The naysayers, whose stronghold is in the north of the country, believe that Norway, with its wealth in oil and gas and its rich fishing grounds, will do just fine without being tied to a Union where environmental and labour standards are significantly lower.

November 28. The Princess of Wales visits a home for underprivileged children in eastern Paris during a one-day trip to France.

Major wins a crucial vote at Westminster

London, Monday 28
John Major, who threatened to go to the country if he lost tonight's vote on increasing Britain's contributions to the EU, duly won by 330 votes to 303, a satisfactory majority of 27. However, determined to impose discipline on his party, the prime minister has ordered the Whip to be withdrawn from eight Tory Euro-rebels – made outcasts in their own party – after they defied his orders to back the Bill. Sir Richard Body, another Euro-rebel, has resigned the Whip even though he voted with the government. This means that the Tories' slim majority of 14 has been slashed to the danger point. The Whipless members are loose cannons, outside party control, and while they may vote with the government on most matters, if they chose to vote with the opposition they could bring Major down.

November 28. Jeffrey Dahmer, serving a life sentence in Wisconsin for murder and cannibalism, is killed by a fellow inmate.

Yeltsin gets tough with Chechen separatists

Fire engulfs ill-fated liner off Somali coast

In Grozny, Chechen leaders say Yeltsin was drunk when he made his threat.

The Achille Lauro, *built in 1947, slowly sinks into the shark-infested ocean.*

Moscow, Tuesday 29
Russian warplanes bombed Grozny, capital of the breakaway Caucasian state of Chechenia, today, signalling President Yeltsin's determination to use force to bring the Chechens back into the Russian fold. The move was apparently prompted by the failure of the Russian-backed opposition to topple General Dzhokar Dudayev, the Chechen leader, in heavy fighting in Grozny at the weekend. Yeltsin threatened today to impose a state of emergency and use "all the forces and means of our state" unless the Chechens "lay down their arms, disband all the armed units within 48 hours". He will need to be careful, for the Chechens are doughty warriors, and he could find himself ensnared in another Afghanistan. (→ 11/12)

Indian Ocean, Wednesday 30
The *Achille Lauro* has captured the world's attention for the last time. A fire that broke out in the engine room is raging through the doomed, slowly sinking ship.

The vessel is notorious for having been hijacked by Palestinian terrorists in 1985. They threw Leon Klinghoffer, a 69-year-old Jewish passenger in a wheelchair, overboard to his death. There was more controversy this spring when the cruise liner was chartered by the Italian neo-fascist National Alliance.

An oil-tanker was the first vessel to respond to the *Achille Lauro*'s distress call. Nearly all of the 979 passengers and crew have been safely evacuated, but at least two people, a Briton and a German, died during the rescue operation. (→ 2/12)

Serbs humiliate UN leader in Sarajevo

Sarajevo, Wednesday 30
UN Secretary General Butros Butros Ghali was snubbed in the most humiliating fashion here today when Radovan Karadzic, the Bosnian Serb leader, refused to meet him during his flying visit to this battered city in an attempt to bring relief to Bihac and to rescue the UN's failing mission in Bosnia. Karadzic's snub stemmed from Ghali's own refusal to accept the Serb as a head of state. The secretary general could not do this without recognising as a legitimate state the territory the Serbs have carved out of Bosnia by force of arms. For that reason, Ghali insisted that their talks take place at the UN-controlled Sarajevo airport; but, in doing so, he made himself vulnerable to the humiliation which Karadzic, a diplomatic street-fighter, duly proceeded to inflict. (→ 8/12)

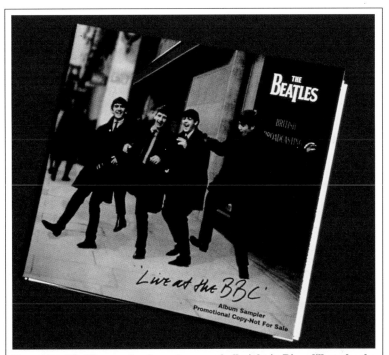

November 30. Thousands of people queued all night in Piccadilly to be the first to buy a copy of the first Beatles album for 24 years, *The Beatles Live at the BBC,* **featuring 56 tracks recorded for radio shows by Liverpool's Fab Four in the early 1960s and resuscitated from the BBC's sound archives.**

Apple's leader bytes into computer dream

New York, Wednesday 30
Promises that new computer technologies will radically change the way we live are so much cyberhype, says Michael Spindler, chairman of Apple Comduter. CD-ROMs of games and books are a huge new market, companies are announcing plans to push their products on the Internet, and mergers of cable television and telephone companies are in the news daily. Even though an information superhighway is being created, and computers continue to grow more powerful and more common, the promises of enthusiastic industry executives are growing too farfetched, says Spindler: "This is not going to be an all-electronic world where we all sit on the couch and are force-fed a constant stream of information." He fears overinflated expectations may lead to a consumer backlash.

December

1994

Su	Mo	Tu	We	Th	Fr	Sa
				1	2	3
4	5	6	7	8	9	10
11	12	13	14	15	16	17
18	19	20	21	22	23	24
25	26	27	28	29	30	31

New York, 1
A special UN commission blames Hutus for the massacre of 500,000 Rwandans earlier this year.

Paris, 1
On World AIDS Day, delegates from 42 nations declare that fighting the disease must be a political priority. (→9)

Berlin, 1
Irmgard Moller, a German terrorist given a life sentence for killing three US soldiers in 1972, is freed.

Indian Ocean, 2
The liner *Achille Lauro* finally sinks.

California, 3
US cyclist Greg LeMond, three-time winner of the Tour de France, retires from the sport.

Moscow, 4
Sweden wins the Davis Cup for the fifth time.

Switzerland, 4
In a referendum, 72.8% of voters back government plans to make granting asylum to foreigners more difficult.

London, 5
Labour's shadow Home Secretary, Jack Straw, calls for a Scandinavian-type monarchy, stripped of all political influence.

Windsor, 6
The Queen gives permission for a Canadian firm to prospect for oil in the grounds of Windsor Castle.

Rome, 6
Antonio Di Pietro, a leading anti-corruption magistrate, resigns. (→22)

Westminster, 8
In a mini-budget, Kenneth Clarke announces an increase in the price of petrol, tobacco and alcohol.

Birmingham, 8
A man stabs 15 shoppers in a store before being arrested.

DEATHS

6. Gian Maria Volonte, Italian film actor (*9/4/33).

8. Antonio Jobim, Brazilian composer (*27/1/27).

10. Lord (Keith) Joseph, British politician (*17/1/18).

'Hollywood Madam' Heidi Fleiss found guilty

Los Angeles, Friday 2
Heidi Fleiss, the 28-year-old woman known as the Hollywood Madam, has been convicted on charges of running a prostitution ring.

Fleiss has claimed her "little black book" of clients contains the names of some of the most famous and powerful men in Hollywood – the "top 1%", as she said. Tinseltown had breathed a sigh of relief when the judge ruled that the names in the book were immaterial to the case. But Fleiss has a talent for self promotion: She has capitalized on her notoriety by selling lingerie and boxer shorts, and after the trial ended today, said: "I don't think I can be quiet about it too much longer, so you will be hearing about the black book."

On trial for running a call-girl ring.

Major suffers tax defeat

Westminster, Tuesday 6
John Major's hapless government stumbled into another humiliation tonight when its plan to increase VAT on fuel to 17.5% was defeated by eight votes. The Labour Party has waged a hard-hitting campaign against the increase, concentrating on the effect it might have on poor old-age pensioners in a harsh winter. Many Tory MPs also disliked the increase, which was unpopular in their constituencies. But, given some vigorous arm-twisting by the Whips and the promise by Chancellor Kenneth Clarke to make £129 million available to ease the pensioners' plight, it was expected that the government would squeeze through. It was the Euro-rebels who decided otherwise. Having had the Whip taken from them last week for voting against an increase in payments to the EU, they set up an ambush. They allowed the government to think they would vote for the fuel tax increase, but six voted against and several abstained. The embarrassed chancellor must now find £1.5 billion from other sources. (→8)

Dec. 1. Queen Elizabeth, who said in October that Manchester was 'not such a nice place', visits the city and confirms that she does like it after all.

Moscow snubs plan to enlarge Alliance

Brussels, Thursday 1
Russian Foreign Minister Andrei Kozyrev threw NATO into confusion tonight by suddenly rejecting the alliance's Partnership for Peace agreement. He had been expected to approve a carefully worked out plan for Russia's participation in the partnership and should also have signed a document setting out the terms of Russia's "broad and enhanced dialogue" with NATO. His refusal to sign after all the preparatory work had been done is apparently in protest at moves to speed the admission of other former Soviet satellites into the alliance. The Russians, it seems, do not want NATO extended to their borders.

AIDS crusader loses fight against disease

Elizabeth and husband 'Starsky'.

Santa Monica, Calif, Saturday 3
Elizabeth Glaser, who became an AIDS activist after learning that she had become infected with HIV from a blood transfusion in 1981 and had passed it on to her son and daughter, died today of the disease at the age of 47. She learned that she had the disease in 1985, when her daughter Ariel, who later died, became seriously ill. Her husband, Paul Glaser, the co-star of the television show *Starsky and Hutch*, is the only member of the family not to have been infected.

Pentagon knew of Gulf War drugs' risk

Washington, Thursday 8

US soldiers in the Persian Gulf were given drugs and vaccines to protect them from Iraqi chemical weapons even though the Pentagon was not sure they were safe. Senator Jay Rockefeller, chairman of the Veterans Affairs Committee, which submitted the report, said: "The investigational drugs and vaccines that were meant to help Gulf troops could have harmed them instead." Physicians from the Department of Veterans Affairs have examined more than 17,000 Gulf vets who suffer from a wide variety of illnesses. They have found no single cause for the ailments but deny that the drugs account for them.

Clinton sees red over masturbation classes

Washington, Friday 9

President Clinton has dismissed the highest-ranking US health official, Joycelen Elders, after she suggested that masturbation should be taught in public schools. The surgeon general made the comment in response to a question as to whether she supported promoting masturbation as a safe-sex activity for school-aged children after her speech at a World AIDS Day conference. Elders had already drawn criticism for saying she supported legalizing drugs.

US to help pull out Bosnia peacekeepers

Serb forces are making life increasingly difficult for UN troops in Bosnia.

Washington, Thursday 8

The United States has agreed "in principle" to send troops to Bosnia to cover the evacuation of the UN peacekeeping forces if it becomes necessary for the "blue helmets" to fight their way out. This could mean the adding of 25,000 combat troops to keep the roads open as the UN units make their way to safety from isolated parts of the hostile country. This change of heart by President Clinton, who has refused to commit ground troops until now, is a welcome move following the fiasco in Budapest on Tuesday when the 52-nation Conference on Security and Cooperation in Europe failed to agree on Bosnia and collapsed in a welter of recrimination. All that the largest gathering of world leaders yet held in Europe could decide was to rename itself the Organization for Security and Cooperation in Europe. (→ 12)

Historic talks get under way in Ulster

Belfast, Friday 9

British officials met representatives of Sinn Fein – one of them a convicted bomber – for their first formal meeting in 22 years at the Stormont Parliament building today. It soon became apparent that the IRA's surrender of its weapons will be a crucial point in the initial talks. Michael Ancram, the minister for Northern Ireland, said a failure to resolve the issue would form "a substantial barrier" to Sinn Fein's entry into the talks to decide Ulster's future. Nevertheless, Ancram said the meeting was "constructive and businesslike", with both sides having "a good trot round the course". Martin McGuinness, leader of the Sinn Fein delegation, said: "We have made a beginning. It should have happened a long time ago. This is a historic opportunity that needs to be built upon." Not everybody agreed: Peter Robinson, deputy leader of the hard-line Democratic Unionists, argued: "The IRA's path to the talks table was by violence. It represents a triumph of terror over the democratic process." (→ 14)

Michael Jordan is best paid sportsman

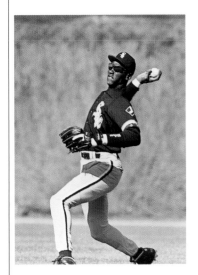

Michael Jordan, former basketball great and now a minor league baseball player, is the world's best paid athlete, according to *Forbes Magazine*. His $10,000 annual salary is well supplemented by $30 million in outside income. Here are the rest of the top 10 (income in millions of dollars):

2. Shaq O'Neal, basketball 16.7
3. Jack Nicklaus, golf   14.8
4. Arnold Palmer, golf   13.6
5. Gerhard Berger, F1   13.5
6. Wayne Gretzky, hockey   13.5
7. Michael Moorer, boxing   12.1
8. Evander Holyfield, boxing 12
9. Andre Agassi, tennis   11.4
10. Nigel Mansell, F1   11.3

Dec. 6. A New York diamond dealer pays $398,500 at Christie's for the bronze statue used in John Huston's 1941 masterpiece, *The Maltese Falcon*.

December

1994

Su	Mo	Tu	We	Th	Fr	Sa
				1	2	3
4	5	6	7	8	9	10
11	12	13	14	15	16	17
18	19	20	21	22	23	24
25	26	27	28	29	30	31

Chechenia, 11
President Yeltsin sends an estimated 30,000 troops and hundreds of tanks into the rebel republic (→ 16).

London, 11
Formula One driver Damon Hill is voted BBC Sports Personality of the Year; athletes Sally Gunnell and Colin Jackson are second and third.

London, 11
Controversy erupts after an unidentified person wins £17.8 million in the National Lottery's first big jackpot.

New York, 12
The UN announces that Major-General Rupert Smith will succeed Lieutenant-General Sir Michael Rose as commander of UN forces in Bosnia on January 24, 1995. (→ 19)

Scotland, 12
Severe flooding in western and central Scotland claims three lives.

Brazil, 12
Former President Fernando Collor is acquitted of corruption charges.

Lisbon, 13
The Duchess of York reveals that she has had two tests for AIDS.

Belfast, 14
John Major announces a £73 million investment package for Northern Ireland. (→ 15)

Dudley, 15
Labour's candidate, Ian Pearson, easily wins the Dudley West by-election.

North Korea, 16
Pyongyang says that a US airman was killed when his OH-58 scout helicopter was shot down after straying across the border.

Bastogne, Belgium, 16
American World War II vets mark the 50th anniversary of the Battle of the Bulge.

Washington, 17
A man fires four shots at the White House. (→ 20)

DEATHS

13. Norman Beaton, British actor (*31/10/34).

13. Antoine Pinay, French statesman (*30/12/1891).

Delors destroys French left's hopes for victory in presidential race

The EU Commission president's decision has left French Socialists in disarray.

Paris, Sunday 11
After weeks of speculation over whether he would run for president of France, Jacques Delors went on television tonight to give his decision. In a short prepared speech, he explained that he would not run because he would not have the support of parliament, which is overwhelmingly conservative, to carry out the programmes he deemed necessary for his country. He seemed to have no doubt he could have won, an opinion backed up by the polls. He also cited personal reasons; his wife is worried about the 69-year-old's health. The spring election will now almost certainly come down to a choice between Prime Minister Edouard Balladur and the Gaullist candidate Jacques Chirac.

Athletics star Diane Modahl is banned for four years for drug-taking

London, Thursday 15
Diane Modahl, the former 800 metres Commonwealth gold medalist, was banned from competing for four years today following tests which showed she had a level of the male hormone testosterone 42 times greater than normal.

The British Athletics Federation disciplinary panel dismissed claims that this could have been caused by mishandling in the Portuguese laboratory where her urine specimen was analysed in June. The panel's decision was unaminous, and it was satisfied "beyond reasonable doubt" of her guilt. Modahl said she was horrified and would appeal.

President Nujoma of Namibia is re-elected

Namibia, Tuesday 13
In the first elections since Namibia won independence from South Africa, voters returned President Sam Nujoma and his South West Africa People's Organization to power.

It was an overwhelming victory, with SWAPO taking 53 of the 72 parliamentary seats and Nujoma winning 73.6% of the vote. The Democratic Turnhalle Alliance took 15 seats, and the United Democratic Front won two. Commonwealth and European observers said the election had been free and fair, but the DTA attempted to freeze the results, alleging voter fraud.

Dec. 14. Jamke Janssen is chosen to play the new James Bond girl.

Chechens defy Russians

Tough Chechen fighters prepare to face Russian tanks heading for Grozny.

Grozny, Friday 16
Boris Yeltsin's invasion of Chechenia is proving to be no walkover. The Chechens are living up to their reputation as guerrilla warriors. Two days ago, they brought down a Russian helicopter with small-arms fire, and today 150 unarmed women brought an armoured column to a halt outside the captial. The commander, General Ivan Babichev, a tough paratrooper, could have easily brushed them aside with his tanks. Instead, he refused to move: "An officer has to obey only legitimate orders," he said. "How can it be lawful to crush civilians under tanks?" He insisted that he was not leading a mutiny, merely following Yeltsin's decree which assured the Chechens that no weapons would be used against civilians. (→ 22)

John Bruton takes over as Ireland's premier

Dublin, Thursday 15
Ireland's bizarre political crisis was resolved today when John Bruton, 47, was elected Taoiseach, or prime minister, at the head of a coalition of his Fine Gael party, the Labour Party and the Democratic Left. It is an amalgam of right and left, and even at the last moment it almost fell apart over the share-out of ministries. Bruton, a barrister, comes from a wealthy farming family and is a right-winger, sneered at as a Thatcherite by his critics. He is still known as "Brutal Bruton", a name he earned by proposing to put VAT on children's shoes when he was finance minister in 1982. More importantly, he is thought to be less sympathetic towards the IRA than his predecessor, Albert Reynolds. The Unionists have given his appointment a guarded welcome. Sinn Fein is said to be uneasy. (→ 23)

Jurassic trees are discovered in Australia

Sydney, Wednesday 14
Scientists at the Royal Botanic Gardens today revealed a discovery they called "the equivalent of finding a small dinosaur still alive on Earth". The exact location of the find, 39 prehistoric pine trees in the Wollemi National Park in the Blue Mountains, is being kept a secret to protect the trees. The oldest of the conifers, which measure 130 feet tall and 10 feet in diameter, are between 200 and 300 years old. Their closest relatives are extinct and are now found only in fossils from the Jurassic and Cretacious periods, about 65 million to 200 million years ago. The scientists call the new genus the Wollemi pine, but the New South Wales environment minister has another name: "It's going to be the Australian Christmas tree."

December 12. As Canova's *The Three Graces* is unveiled, Elizabeth Esteve-Coll, the director of the Victoria and Albert Museum who played a major role in saving the masterpiece for the nation, announces her resignation.

Dec. 13. The death last year in Paris of Germaine Krebs (*30/11/03), known throughout the fashion world as Madame Grès, the last grande dame of haute couture, is revealed after having been kept secret by her daughter.

December

1994

Su	Mo	Tu	We	Th	Fr	Sa
				1	2	3
4	5	6	7	8	9	10
11	12	13	14	15	16	17
18	19	20	21	22	23	24
25	26	27	28	29	30	31

Southampton, 18
Angry passengers who were unable to join the *QE2*'s Christmas cruise because of unfinished work aboard the liner form an action group to sue Cunard. (→ 25)

Cuba, 18
According to a poll, a majority of Cubans still support Fidel Castro and blame the US for the island's economic woes.

Sydney, 18
Cricketer Brian Lara, who holds the world record for the highest Test innings, is dismissed for 23 by a woman bowler during a charity match.

London, 19
Rolls-Royce announce that BMW will supply V-8 and V-12 engines to power their cars.

Washington, 20
Secret Service officers kill a knife-wielding man outside the White House. (→ 25)

New York, 20
The BBC announces the launch next February of a 24-hour news cable television service in the US.

Prague, 20
Czech police say they have seized 6.6 pounds of smuggled weapons-grade uranium.

Britain, 21
An opinion poll shows that support for John Major's government has sunk to its lowest level ever: just 8%.

Berlin, 22
Ministers from Belgium, France, Germany, Portugal, Spain, Luxembourg and the Netherlands agree to end border controls on March 26 next year.

London, 22
Britain's trade balance registers a surplus for the first time since 1987.

Dublin, 23
Nine convicted IRA members are released from Irish jails on Christmas parole.

DEATHS

18. Lord (David) Pitt of Hampstead, Labour politician (*3/10/13).

20. Dean Rusk, US statesman (*9/2/09).

Jimmy Carter gets Serb leaders to agree to four-month ceasefire

The former American president and the Bosnian Serb leader, Radovan Karadzic, announce the agreement in Pale.

Sarajevo, Monday 19
Former US President Jimmy Carter appears to have brought off a surprising coup. He emerged from several hours of talks in the Bosnian Serb stronghold of Pale today with an offer of a four-month ceasefire from the normally intractable Serb leader, Radovan Karadzic. While the Serbs seem to have granted few concessions to this innocent in the maelstrom of Bosnian politics, Carter, his famous grin firmly in place, said they had "agreed to an immediate ceasefire and to negotiate a lasting cessation of hostilities. While a ceasefire is in place, Bosnian Serb leaders agree to discuss peace on the Contact Group plan at a mutually acceptable site."

Carter is due to return to Sarajevo tonight to present the Serb offer to the Bosnian government. UN officials welcome the offer of a ceasefire but fear that Karadzic is using the former president and his reputation for making peace to champion the Serb initiative on the international stage, enabling them to freeze the current front lines. This would allow them to keep a grip on all their gains and establish their own state in 70% of Bosnia. (→ 25)

Dec. 21. Rescuers examine the wreckage of an Air Algérie Boeing 737 cargo plane that narrowly missed a housing estate before crashing on a wood during its approach to Coventry's Baginton Airport, killing all five people on board.

Silvio Berlusconi resigns

Russian bombers intensify attacks on Grozny

The Italian premier could not hang on after his coalition government collapsed.

Chechen women plead with a Russian soldier to allow them to flee to safety.

Rome, Thursday 22

Italy is in political crisis today after Prime Minister Silvio Berlusconi submitted his resignation to President Oscar Luigi Scalfaro rather than face a no-confidence vote. Now the president must decide whether to call new elections soon or to appoint a new premier at the head of a transitional government which would undertake electoral reform before a new poll. Berlusconi, who will act as caretaker premier until the president has decided, wants spring elections, while his one-time coalition partner and now political nemesis, Umberto Bossi of the Northern League, wants the parliament to undertake electoral reform before Italians vote for a new government, a view which is said to be shared by the president.

Grozny, Thursday 22

Wave after wave of Russian jets screamed over Grozny, the capital of the breakaway state of Chechenia, raining bombs and rockets onto the undefended city today while artillery lobbed shells into its streets. Terrified inhabitants fled to the hills. It appears that the Russians are relying on their air force to break Chechen resistance as army generals show growing reluctance to risk the lives of their men or order the slaughter of Chechen civilians. Three generals from the North Caucasus Military District are reported to have been fired for "indecisiveness and inaction", and Colonel-General Eduard Vorobyov, deputy commander of land forces, has resigned rather than take charge of the unpopular operation. (→ 25)

Angry young man John Osborne dies

Shropshire, Saturday 24

Actor and playwright John Osborne (*12/12/29), who made his mark as a dramatist with the play *Look Back in Anger*, died in hospital here today. His anti-hero, Jimmy Porter, was immediately recognised as the archetype of the disillusioned youth of the 50s, and Osborne was labelled an "angry young man", along with Kingsley Amis and the other writers who decried the ills of post-war British society and used a realistic style dubbed the "kitchen sink" genre. But as the years went on, they became absorbed into the establishment like so many other rebels. Osborne scored further successes with *The Entertainer* and *Inadmissible Evidence*. He married five times and was a prodigious drinker.

Dec. 22. Eurotunnel's first fare-paying passengers drive their cars onto Le Shuttle at Folkestone prior to the train's departure for France at 10:09am. The travellers arrived on time after a 35 minute trip through the Channel Tunnel.

December

Washington, 25
Police arrest an unarmed man who had climbed on top of the White House fence.

South Pole, 25
A 41-year-old Norwegian, Liv Arnesen, celebrates after becoming the first woman to trek to the South Pole alone.

Jerusalem, 25
Thirteen people are injured, some of them severely, when explosives carried by an Islamic Resistance Movement suicide bomber blow up, killing the terrorist.

Sarajevo, 25
President Alija Izetbegovic of Bosnia threatens a resumption of fighting unless attacks on the Bihac pocket cease.

Baghdad, 25
As President Saddam Hussein again calls for international sanctions to be lifted, the US Navy stops and boards a Honduras-registered ship, the *Ajmir*, suspected of violating the UN trade embargo on Iraq.

Washington, 26
The Food and Drug Administration approves the first AIDS test that uses saliva instead of blood to determine whether a patient has contracted the disease.

Moscow, 26
President Yeltsin offers to open peace talks with Chechen leaders, but Russian Deputy Prime Minister Nikolai Yegorov says the rebels must be crushed.

United States, 27
Medical researchers claim that mistletoe can be used to treat some cases of lung cancer.

Jerusalem, 30
The Jewish Agency says that some 78,000 immigrants, approximately 66,000 of them from the former Soviet Union, settled in Israel this year.

Geneva, 31
At midnight tonight, the World Trade Organization, which succeeds the General Agreement on Tariffs and Trade, is born.

DEATH

25. Zail Singh, former president of India (*5/5/16).

Yeltsin's forces continue bid to pound Chechens into submission

Moscow, Sunday 25
As bombs rained down on Grozny today, Sergei Kovalyov, the Russian human rights commissioner, called on Boris Yeltsin to halt his offensive against the Chechens and suggested that the Russian president is being manipulated by his security chiefs. In a telegram addressed to Yeltsin, he says: "You must understand that you are losing time. ... Those who started the war will very soon not need you. Only you are capable of stopping this crazy massacre and of pulling the nation out of this vicious circle of despair and blood-stained lies." Yeltsin is keeping silent, but his ministers remain determined to carry on the attack.

Meanwhile in Grozny, the Chechen leader, General Dudayev, remains defiant despite the Russian ground offensive this weekend in which the Kremlin claims to have killed 1,000 rebels. (→ 26)

General Dzhokar Dudayev, the Chechen leader, says he will fight to the end.

Passengers threaten legal action over Cunard's 'cruise from hell'

Atlantic Ocean, Sunday 25
Passengers on the *QE2* are trying to enjoy Christmas and forget the disasters of the past few days that have led some of them to rebaptize the cruise liner a "floating Bosnia". The problems stem from a £30 million refitting of the vessel earlier this year. Hundreds of passengers were turned away eight days ago when the *QE2* left Southampton for New York because their berths were not ready. Some of them are threatening to sue, although Cunard has offered compensation. After the liner arrived in New York, it was held up by the US Coast Guard, which had found fire and safety violations. Repairs were hastily carried out, and the ship set sail. Because of the delays, the cruise has skipped calls in Fort Lauderdale and the Caribbean island of St Martin – stops that were to be highlights of the trip.

Queen calls for peace in Christmas speech

Europe: And then there were fifteen

Windsor, Sunday 25

The Queen's traditional Christmas broadcast was one of hope today. She spoke of the commemoration of the D-Day landings and then talked about the new dawn of peace in the modern world: "If that new dawn is to be a real, and not a false one, courage, patience and faith will be sorely needed – those same qualities which kept the flame of hope alive in the war-torn countries of Europe and the Far East in the dark days of the last war." She said that Christ had taught us to love our enemies and continued: "This year we have seen shining examples of that generosity of spirit which alone can banish division and prejudice. In Northern Ireland, peace is gradually taking root; a fully democratic South Africa has been welcomed back into the Commonwealth; and, in the Middle East, long-standing enmities are healing. ... A Happy Christmas and God bless you."

Brussels, Saturday 31

At midnight tonight, the European Union will gain three more members, Austria, Finland and Sweden, bringing the membership up to 15.

It should have been 16, but last month the Norwegians voted "no", and the Swedes almost joined them in isolation with a vote in which the "yes" camp polled at 52% against the 47% "no" vote. But the majority wins, and tonight 22 million more Europeans will find themselves committed to rule from Brussels, exchanging a loss of sovereignty for membership of the world's largest economic alliance.

Since the European Economic Community came into being 37 years ago, it has grown in size and in ambition, with France and Germany working for a single currency and a federal Europe. The United Kingdom remains intensely sceptical about all such developments and may yet decide by referendum to refuse to take part in them.

French commandos kill Algerian hijackers

Marseilles, Monday 26

The four Algerian Islamic extremists who hijacked an Air France Airbus in Algiers have been killed in a commando raid on the plane here. The A300 was commandeered Saturday, and the hijackers demanded to fly to France. After a 40-hour stand-off in Algiers, where three hostages were killed, the plane flew here.

Freed passengers said the terrorists' plan was to fly on to Paris and crash the plane. The anti-terrorist team made its attack at 5:15pm. About 30 commandos stormed the jet, and others helped hostages escape. The operation was not a total success: Of the 173 passengers, 13 were injured, as were three crew members and nine commandos.

A helmeted French commando fires at the terrorists in the aircraft's cockpit.

MAN OF THE YEAR

TIME

POPE

January 13, Johan Holst

Johan Holst was Norway's foreign minister for less than 10 months but assured his place in history by leading the secret Israel-PLO talks that led to their 1993 peace accord.

January 23, Brian Redhead

Anchorman of Radio 4's *Today* programme, Redhead, a feisty northerner, became familiar to millions of listeners through his abrasive early morning duels with politicians.

February 6, Joseph Cotten

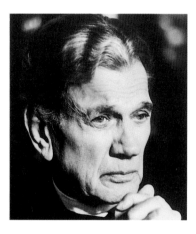

Joseph Cotten, a master of both the silver screen and the Broadway stage, gained fame in Welles's *Citizen Kane* and starred in Hitchcock's *Shadow of a Doubt*. His Broadway appearances included *The Philadelphia Story* and *Sabrina Fair*.

February 19, Derek Jarman

Jarman, who died of AIDS, had just finished *Blue*, a film consisting of his personal commentary on the progression of his illness. His films include *Sebastiane* and *Jubilee*.

February 24, Dinah Shore

American singer and film actress Dinah Shore was one of the few women to host a variety show in television's early days. Her TV career continued into the early 1990s.

February 27, Harold Acton

Sir Harold was an expert on Italian art, an art historian and an avid collector. He left La Pietra, his Italian estate, with its valuable art collection, to New York University.

March 4, John Candy

Canadian-born John Candy acted and wrote for the TV comedy show *Second City TV* before going on to star in the blockbuster *Home Alone* and *Cool Runnings*, a film about the Jamaican bobsled team.

March 9, Fernando Rey

The Spanish actor made four films with his compatriot Luis Buñuel, including *The Discreet Charm of the Bourgeoisie*. He also gained much praise for his work in the American thriller *The French Connection*.

March 9, Charles Bukowski

Hard-drinking and rough-talking Henry Chinaski was Bukowski's alter ego in his novels *Notes of a Dirty Old Man* and *Post Office*. The film *Barfly* dramatized his younger days.

March 15, Mai Zetterling

Swedish-born Zetterling became a film star after World War II but gave up acting to direct in the 1960s. Her feminist films include *Loving Couples*, *The Girls* and *Scrubbers*.

April 1, Robert Doisneau

Robert Doisneau is perhaps the photographer most associated with Paris. His most famous photograph, "Le Baiser de l'Hôtel de Ville", two lovers on a busy street, typifies the romantic idea of the city.

April 27, Lynne Frederick

Actress Lynne Frederick achieved fame and heartache as the fourth and last wife of manic comedian Peter Sellers. He left her £4 million, and she spent it all, seeking happiness in drink.

April 30, Richard Scarry

Scarry wrote and illustrated children's books which have sold more than 100 million copies around the world. His 250 books have been translated into dozens of languages.

May 24, John Wain

Professor of poetry at Oxford, Wain was also a critic and anthologist. His first novel, *Hurry on Down*, made his name, and his biography of Samuel Johnson was widely acclaimed.

May 29, Erich Honecker

Honecker ruled East Germany for 18 years, until the *Wende* (change) of 1989. The ruthless dictator spent his final days in Chile, having escaped being tried for treason in Germany because of poor health.

June 14, Henry Mancini

Mancini, Hollywood's best known composer of music for films and television, scored *Peter Gunn*, *The Pink Panther* and *Breakfast at Tiffany's*, in which Audrey Hepburn sang his most popular song, "Moon River".

the many who died in 1994

July 2, Marion Williams
Marion Williams was one of the greatest of gospel singers. She debuted with the Ward Singers in the 1940s and went on to achieve international acclaim as a soloist.

July 17, Jean Borotra

The "Bounding Basque" was part of the "Musketeers", the French tennis team that won the Davis Cup six consecutive times from 1927 to 1932. He won six Wimbledon titles and was the French champion 60 times.

July 31, Caitlin Thomas
Caitlin, widow of the Welsh poet Dylan Thomas, matched her husband in infidelity and was an even fiercer drinker than he. She published a memoir of their life in 1982.

September 6, James Clavell

Australian-born Clavell specialized in novels about the Far East. His latest, *Gai-Jin*, is a bestseller; *Shogun* was made into a TV miniseries. He also wrote such popular films as *To Sir, with Love* and *The Great Escape*.

September 7, Terence Young

Terence Young directed the first two James Bond films, *Dr No* and *To Russia with Love*, setting the series' sophisticated and fast-paced style. His wide-ranging oeuvre also encompassed French and Italian art films.

September 17, Karl Popper
The Austrian-born philosopher was a prominent anti-communist voice, and his views helped shape the Conservative government's ideology in the Thatcher years.

September 18, Vitas Gerulaitis

Tennis player Gerulaitis won the Australian Open in 1977 and was ranked in the top 10 from that year until 1983. He enjoyed the night life and was an habitué of New York's Studio 54 in the late 1970s.

September 20, Jule Styne
The London-born composer wrote thousands of songs, hundreds of which were hits, including "Diamonds are a Girl's Best Friend" and "Everything's Coming Up Roses".

September 23, Madeleine Renaud

France's leading actress for six decades, Renaud debuted at the *Comédie française* at 21. The company she formed in 1940 with her husband, Jean-Louis Barrault, produced plays until his death in January.

September 27, Harry Saltzman
Saltzman produced the Broadway and film versions of Osborne's *Look Back in Anger* before teaming up with Albert "Cubby" Broccoli to produce the James Bond film series.

October 24, Raul Julia

Julia, a star of New York theatre on and off Broadway before his cinema career, starred in 1985's *Kiss of the Spider Woman* and played Gomez, the patriarch of Charles Addams's cartoon family, in the 1991 film.

October 31, John Pope-Hennessy
Sir John, an authority on the Italian Renaissance, was the only person to have been director of both the Victoria and Albert Museum and the British Museum.

November 10, Carmen McRae
McRae, hailed by the US National Endowment for the Arts as a "master of jazz", was a pianist as well as a singer and one of the best known women performers in the genre.

November 18, Cab Calloway

Calloway, the boisterous big band leader, served as the model for the character Sportin' Life in *Porgy and Bess*. The best known of his swinging and humorous songs is "Minnie the Moocher", his first big hit.

December 6, Gian Maria Volonte

Volonte's most critically acclaimed work was in films such as *The Moro Affair*, which reflected his interest in Italian politics, but he is more famous in Britain for his roles in Sergio Leone's spaghetti westerns.

December 10, Keith Joseph
Lord Joseph, a Tory MP from 1956 to 1987, helped form his party's free-market policies. Margaret Thatcher considered him a mentor and one of her most important advisors.

118

119

Picture Index

The position of the illustrations is indicated by letters: t = top, b = bottom, r = right, l = left, m = middle, x = middle left, y = middle right.